English
Language
Games

English Language Games

Activities for developing vocabulary,
expression, imagination, powers of
deduction, and skills of articulation

Christine Purkis
and
Cathy Guérin

Macmillan Education
London and Basingstoke

To all our guinea-pigs

First published 1984

Published by
MACMILLAN EDUCATION LIMITED
Houndmills, Basingstoke, Hampshire RG21 2XS
and London

Companies and representatives throughout the world

Typesetting in Souvenir by Vine & Gorfin Ltd, Exmouth
Printed in Hong Kong

ISBN 0 333 34965 2

CONTENTS

LANGUAGE GAMES

Introduction

STIMULUS TO WRITING

Introduction

ACKNOWLEDGEMENTS

The authors and publishers wish to thank Little, Brown & Co. for permission to reproduce 'The Secret in the Cat' from *New and Selected Things Taking Place* by May Swenson, Copyright © 1964 by May Swenson.

The exercise on page 92 is based on one in *Making Sense of Comprehension* by Mike Hamlin and David Jackson (Macmillan Education, 1984).

INTRODUCTION

The 'games' format is gaining increasing currency as a learning medium: not because it is necessarily more 'fun' than traditional learning situations, and certainly not because it introduces any competitiveness or 'winners'. The games medium works in a number of curriculum areas because it sets specific objectives, and limited parameters, within which prescribed tasks can be played out in collaborative groups, without constant surveillance by the teacher.

It is for this reason that the teaching of English also lends itself to a games approach. Under specific headings of Oral, Language, Writing and Reading games, a series of situations are offered in which incentives are set up for developing vocabulary, expression, imagination, powers of deduction and skills of articulation.

The ability levels for which these games are appropriate can vary immensely, hence the indications of age and ability at the foot of each game. The sequence suggests a progression in difficulty within each section. Special attention has been given to the needs of slow learners, but at the same time many of the games can equally well be played at quite a sophisticated level.

Please do not relegate these games to a Friday afternoon: their value lies in their use for lesson starters, group organisation and as aids for non-specialist supply teachers who need to be sure that their lessons have a failure-proof structure and sound educational objectives. They are equally valuable as a rewarding activity for the end of a hard-working day. Children enjoy games!

ORAL GAMES

Oral skills in English are now at last recognised as being of equal importance to written skills – both in the criteria for new examinations and in general training for the world of work. Directed practice in oral skills has been neglected in the classroom for too long.

The games in the oral section follow a careful progression. The first section, of guessing games, aims to loosen up the pupils' articulation in general participation exercises. Guessing games will be especially appropriate for slow learners, who need to start with simple concentration and quick rewards for success.

We then progress to more protracted, but still closely directed, games: speaking exercises with a definite purpose, to particular audiences, based on specific objectives.

The oral skills section requires far more open-ended expression, introducing the objectives of description, persuasion, reporting, instruction.

Finally, the narrative section of oral games demands extended speech by single pupils in turn, both imaginative and for a directed purpose.

Throughout the oral games it should be stressed that oral ability includes listening ability; each game requires a two-way participation by the players.

One of the most important aspects of oral games is that pupils who find written work difficult can often make an important spoken contribution. Frequently it is through the spoken word that social integration in the classroom is most successful.

1 GUESSING GAMES

Cock-a-doodle-doo

Aim

To make the connection between spoken and written sounds, and to introduce the idea of onomatopoeia.

Requirements

Blackboard, chalk: a tape of sound effects can be prepared for the second part of the game.

Method

Begin by giving simple examples of words which represent sounds.

e.g.: 'Cock-a-doodle-doo' is what a cockerel says in England, but 'Kikiriki'... in France. Does a sheep say, 'Baaa'? Does a cat say, 'Miaow'?

Ask the pupils to choose an animal and write down the sound as accurately as they can, using letters to represent the sound. They should then be asked individually to write their sound on the blackboard, and the rest of the class should guess what animal sound is being represented.

A tape of sound effects may be used and the pupils asked to create the noise in letters, e.g. a train going through a tunnel, a car accident, a fight, etc.

Age   9–11 years. Can be appropriate for slow learners.

Time

This can take a full lesson, or can be used more briefly in conjunction with other methods of teaching letter values.

Moods

Aim

To help pupils to modify their expression according to mood. It is grammatically similar to the 'Adverb Game' but emphasises the oral aspect of the exercise.

Requirements   None.

Method

Divide the class into groups of four, five or six. Each group chooses a word of the same number of letters as members of their group, e.g. a group of five might choose the word 'HORSE'. Each member of the group takes one letter and then chooses a mood or adverb that starts with that letter,

e.g.: 'H' chooses 'hurriedly'
      'O' chooses 'openly'
      'R' chooses 'rudely'
      'S' chooses 'slowly'
      'E' chooses 'excitedly'

Each group in turn sits at the front of the class in order:
H O R S E and the rest of the class ask questions of individual members which must be answered in that mood. The class then guess each mood until they have built the whole word. (N.B. The questions do not ask the pupils for movement, but for variation in oral expression according to the mood.)

e.g.: 'What did you have for breakfast?' is asked of the first pupil and is answered in a 'hurried' manner.

It might be a good idea to say that a minimum of three questions is asked before any guessing takes place, as the best performances may be guessed rather quickly. The class may guess the whole word, but they still have to go on to guess the individual moods.

Age   9–12 years, especially slow learners.

Time   A lesson.

Armchair hide and seek

Aim

To exercise the pupils' power to reason and question and draw deductions. This is a simple non-competitive game where each contribution is valid. It encourages the class to work corporately in reaching the final deduction.

Requirements   None.

Method

Ask for a volunteer who is asked to choose a hiding place where they could just conceivably be, e.g.: On the top of Nelson's Column. The rest of the class must attempt to discover the hiding place by asking questions which elicit only a 'yes/no' answer. The aim is to discover the hiding place in the least possible number of questions.

Age   9–12 years, especially slow learners.

Time

5–10 minutes each guess, extended as long as concentration lasts.

Coffee-pot

Aim

To encourage oral work and socialisation in the class, and to exercise powers of deduction. It can also be used to teach the function of the noun.

Requirements   None.

Method

Ask a pair of volunteers to leave the room to choose a noun, then ask them back to have a conversation about it in front of the class. When they talk, however, they will substitute the word 'coffee-pot' for the chosen word,

e.g.: The pair has chosen the word 'dustbin'. The conversation might go as follows:
'My coffee-pot's black and made of plastic.'
'My coffee-pot's grey but it smells awful.'

When anyone else thinks they know what the 'coffee-pot" is, they may guess. If they are correct, another pair is sent out.

Age   9–12 years, especially slow learners.

Time   10–15 minutes.

Illusions

Aim

To promote class involvement. This game also requires that each pupil knows the difference between a vowel and a consonant.

Requirements   None.

Method

A volunteer is required. It is essential that the teacher chooses a pupil who will react well to this kind of exposure.

The volunteer is told that the class will construct a story in their absence and that this story will be reconstructed by questioning by the volunteer.

The volunteer can only ask direct questions requiring 'Yes' or 'No' answers from the class.

As soon as the pupil leaves the room, the teacher informs the rest of the class that in fact the story is that which the volunteer will create.

The teacher then informs the class that they must answer 'Yes' to all questions ending with a vowel, and 'No' to all questions ending with a consonant,

e.g.: Volunteer: Is it a story about an animal?
　　　 Class: No.
　　　 Volunteer: Is it a story about a house?
　　　 Class: Yes... and so on.

Development

There can of course be several other code variations which can be used apart from vowels and consonants.

Age   9–13 years.

Time

A short game, the length of which is determined by the volunteer's deductive abilities. The teacher may need to drop clues.

N.B. This game can only be played once with any one group.

Just the job

Aim

To identify with various jobs and occupations, leading pupils on from the obvious stereotypes, e.g. a traffic warden writing out a ticket.

Requirements   None.

Method

Each pupil in the class thinks of an unusual job is questioned by the rest of the class about what the job is. The person questioned can only answer 'Yes' or 'No'.

Eventually, if the class cannot guess the job the person has to mime it.

Age   9-13 years, including slow learners.

Time   10-15 minutes.

Trademarks

Aim

To exercise reasoning power and to improve questioning technique. This game is closely linked with 'Just the job' in that it is another questioning and deducing game. One important development is that the pupils have to work in pairs and co-operate in creating their roles.

Requirements   None.

Method

Ask pupils to form pairs, one pair volunteering to start the game.

One of each pair must choose to be a famous person, alive or dead, fictional or real, and the other pupil must choose to be an object associated with that person, e.g. Princess Anne and her horse.

The rest of the class attempts to crack the identity of the person first, aiming to do so in twenty questions with only 'yes/no' answers. When they have used the twenty questions allotted, they move on to question the object.

Variations

Instead of an object, this game works well with a person and a characteristic, e.g. John McEnroe and his temper.

Age   11–13 years, including slow learners.

Time   10–15 minutes.

'B' for Botticelli

Aim

To develop logic and deduction; particularly suitable for smaller groups of pupils.

Requirements   None.

Method

One pupil, 'A', must think of a well-known personality and tell the rest of the class the initial of the surname,

e.g.: 'A' (thinking 'Keegan'): 'The person I am thinking of begins with "K".'

Everybody in the class must try to think of a famous person whose name begins with 'K'. When someone, 'B', has thought of one they may ask an indirect question,

e.g.: If they have thought of Kitchener, they do not ask directly, 'Is it Kitchener?', but obliquely, e.g. 'Is it a general from the First World War famous for his recruiting campaign?'

If 'A' cannot think of any well-known general whose surname begins with 'K' then 'B' has first to reveal whom he or she was thinking of, i.e., Lord Kitchener. Then 'B' can ask 'A' a direct question which needs only a 'Yes' or 'No' answer,

e.g.: 'Are you alive today?' 'A' must answer 'Yes', which is the first clue to the real personality.

However, if 'A' does think of Kitchener then another person from the class comes forward with their suggestion,

e.g.: 'C' (thinking King Kong): 'Is it a big gorilla?' and so on until the true identity is guessed.

Age   14–18 years.

Time   A lesson.

N.B. This game sounds more complicated than it is in practice. It is well worth the effort to master it.

2 DIRECTED SPEECH

Yes or no

Aim

To develop questioning technique, and the art of paraphrase.

Requirements   None.

Method

Explain to the class that the object of the game is for the person being questioned NOT to answer 'Yes' or 'No' and for the people questioning to frame questions in such a way as to try to elicit a 'Yes' or 'No' answer.

Ask for a volunteer to be questioned and then ask the others to begin the grilling. If anyone reaches a full minute without saying the forbidden words they gain a point.

It is fun for the pupils to try this on the teacher, too.

Age   9–12 years, especially slow learners.

Time   10–15 minutes.

Blue moon crackers

Aim

To enjoy free association of words. This can be a useful introduction to simple poetic writing.

Requirements   None.

Method

STAGE ONE   Begin by going round the class with each pupil calling out a word that has some obvious association with the preceding word.

e.g.: BLUE... SKY... AEROPLANE... CLOUDS... RAIN... UMBRELLA, etc.

STAGE TWO   The game is now played with the exact opposite intention, that is, each word must have no connection with the word preceding.
   If any other pupil can see a connection, a challenge can be made and the connection pointed out.

e.g.: TURNIP... HAIRCLIP... TOENAIL... SCISSORS (Challenge: You use scissors to cut toenails.)

Variations

This game can be useful for poetic writing on themes of colour, seasons, and so on,

e.g. Theme Colour – RED

The teacher may encourage distinctions between concrete and abstract manifestations of the colour.

e.g.: **Concrete** associations with RED might be fire, blood, roses, etc.
   Abstract associations may include warmth, love, danger, anger, pain, etc.

Ideas collected in the form of a game can be reorganised carefully into a more poetic, less random sequence.

Age   9–13 years, including slow learners.

Time   10 minutes.

Enquiries

Aim

To develop questioning techniques and the art of framing
constructive questions.

Requirements   Paper and a pen for each pupil.

Method

STAGE ONE   This game begins orally. The pupils are asked to form
pairs, and one of the pair begins the questioning. Instead of
answering with a statement, the question must be parried with
another question.
    The point of the game is to ask as many questions as possible,
and the person wins who lasts the longest.

e.g.: 'What's on at the pictures tonight?'
      'Aren't they doing a series of horror films at the moment?'
      'Yeah, did you see that one about the Elephant Man?'
      'Do you know it took John Hurt five hours to be made up to
      look like that?'
      'I suppose you can hardly call that a horror film, can you?'
      and so on.

STAGE TWO   *Extension into written work:* the questions can be
exchanged on paper, starting a new line for each change of speaker
and putting in the speech marks and question marks accurately.

Age   11–13 years.

Time   10 minutes.

Strike a light

Aim

To provide an oral approach to homonyms: words which sound the same but are spelled differently, or have different meanings. This game can be used as an introduction to written work, or as a correction ploy for common spelling errors.

Requirements   None.

Method

The class should divide into pairs, and each pair should think of a good homonym,

e.g.: fare (price or food), fair (beautiful), fair (just), fair (blonde).

Group the class in a circle leaving a space in the centre for each pair to sit in turn. Each pair must have a conversation about the various meanings of their word, but should avoid mentioning the actual word,

e.g.: 'I went to a really good one last Whitsun.'
      'And I paid a really high one going into Bristol this week-end.'

When another member of the circle thinks that they have guessed the word, they may join in the conversation,

e.g.: 'There is a lot of this kind of person in our class, isn't there?'

If their sentence is accepted by the original two they may join them in the centre and say, 'Strike a light'. If any lights are not struck by the end of a reasonable period of time, the teacher can make the solution very obvious, or tell the rest of the circle still sitting in the dark.

After one homonym has been solved, another pair takes a turn in the centre of the circle.

Age   12–13 years.

Time   A lesson, or lesson-filler.

Railway carriage game

Aim

To practise quick thinking in controlled speech; also careful listening; and to develop convincing role-play.

Requirements   None.

Method

Select two volunteers to wait outside. The rest of the class have to think of two well-known phrases, slogans, proverbs or lines of a well-known song, etc., one for each of the two pupils outside. The first person is called in and given one of the phrases, e.g. 'It never rains but it pours'.

They then each become a character sitting in a railway carriage. The second person is then told their phrase outside the door, e.g. 'Beans means Heinz'.

They also come in, assume a character, and sit down in the carriage. Both characters have to talk to each other, attempting surreptitiously to slip in their phrase as a natural part of the conversation, while trying to spot the other person's.

A time limit of two minutes makes it more interesting.

Age   14–18 years.

Time   A lesson, if each pair has a turn.

N.B. 1 The game may be complicated to explain at first, but it is very worthwhile and pupils find it engrossing.
   2 This game is most successful with pupils who are confident in drama, rather than academically gifted.

Contact

Aim To increase sensory awareness and descriptive skills.

Requirements

Large bag, like a plastic holder, full of objects of different textures. Pupils can be asked in advance to bring an object each.

Method

Either blindfold each pupil in turn or ask the class to hold their hands behind their backs. They must select an object from the bag and touch it, but not look at it. They must make sure that no one from the class sees the object, either. The object must be described in great detail and the rest of the class may guess the identity of the object.

Variations

This game can be developed into writing, where pupils are given an object to describe, and they can then use tactile perceptions as well as other forms of sensory awareness. (See 'What am I?' in the Stimulus to Writing section.)

Age 9–11 years, including slow learners.

Time 10–15 minutes.

N.B. This game is particularly designed for children who are not fluent in writing or speaking.

How to get there

Aim   To practise giving and receiving instructions.

Requirements   Paper and a pen for each pupil.

Method

The class is divided into pairs. One pupil in each pair takes paper
and a pen and draws a map which illustrates the instructions being
given to the other child.

The other pupil, without looking at the map, will give clear
instructions of how to get from the school, for example, to their
home; or from that classroom to the school hall; or from the school
to the local newsagent; and so on.

The pupils then exchange roles and when both maps have been
drawn the results can be discussed.

Age   9–14 years, including slow learners.

Time   A lesson.

Instructions

Aim

To encourage pupils to speak precisely, saying what they mean.

Requirements Blackboard and chalk.

Method

Station one volunteer at the front of the class by the blackboard and another at the back of the class. The person at the back thinks of an object, e.g. bus, hedgehog, cigarette.

The latter then instructs the person at the board what to draw, using only the names of shapes and giving instructions about direction and length of lines. The pupil must NOT say, 'Draw an egg'. They must say, 'Draw an oval', etc. The pupil may not gesticulate, and could be asked to hold their hands firmly behind their back.

The rest of the class watch what is being drawn on the board and guess what it is. If they guess correctly, they may change places with the person calling the instructions, who then exchanges places with the drawer at the board. In this way each pupil should have experience of answering instructions and giving them.

The drawer at the front must not ask questions but must only interpret the instructions. They may correct the drawing only following instructions from the pupil at the back.

Age 9-14 years.

Time

Can be used as a short game (about 15 minutes) or can be extended to fill a whole lesson.

Patent

Aim

To stimulate pupils to talk persuasively and to inspire confidence and the ability to speak fluently in front of a group of their peers.

Requirements

Paper and a pen for each pupil.

Method

Each pupil is asked to create a labour-saving device. They may make notes and draw diagrams to help them in creating their device.

Each pupil should be encouraged to highlight the particular advantages of their device. They should make up a name for it and prepare a speech designed to 'sell' the product to a critical audience.

When the pupils are ready – possibly after a homework of preparation – the group should gather and each pupil in turn is asked to introduce their device. The rest of the class can ask questions about the device after the speech has been delivered.

At the end of the session, votes can be taken for the most ingenious device and for the most persuasive speech.

Age

12–14 years.

Time

This game is best played with time allowed for a planning stage before the oral part of the game is delivered.

Persuasion

Aim

To develop the art of subliminal persuasion, and the ability to detect it!

Requirements   None.

Method

Divide the class into pairs: 'A's and 'B's. All the 'A's decide with the teacher on an activity or a phrase that their partners must be enticed to do or say,

e.g.: scratch your head, or say, 'Bangers and mash'.

All the 'A's have to attempt, subtly, to induce their partners to do the activity,

e.g.: In the first case:
    'A': 'I like your hair: have you had it done recently?
    'Is that bit supposed to stick up like that?'
    Or in the second case:
    'A': 'I wish school dinners would improve, don't you?
       'In fact, I'm going to draw up a menu that we would like. Have you any suggestions?'

Variations

This game can be made more complicated by combining actions and words, for example.

Age   14–16 years.

Time   10–15 minutes.

N.B. Possible development could include work on advertising, looking at persuasive techniques in the media, shops, etc.

The reporting game

Aim

To practise observation and description, and to demonstrate how different versions of an event naturally develop.

Requirements

Reporters and editors will need notebooks and pens or pencils.

Method

The class is split into various groups. One small group prepares a short action-packed mime of a crime, e.g. a bank robbery.

Meanwhile, eight pupils are sent outside: four reporters and four editors. They are paired off so that each editor has a reporter working for him or her. In their pairs they should discuss the type of paper they both work for.

The mime group informs the rest of the class of the time and place and perform the scene. The rest of the class are eyewitnesses and watch carefully.

When the mime is finished the teacher calls the four reporters in. Each reporter chooses two eyewitnesses (one after the other) from the class and questions them about the crime they have seen. The questioning should only take one minute each. The teacher will have to time this.

When the reporters' two minutes are up the teacher then calls the editors in. The reporters each go to their own editor and relate the information they have gleaned from the eyewitnesses. The editors then have another two minutes to write as sensible an account as possible without consulting anyone else.

The editors then read out their 'stories' including headlines, the name of the paper, and so on to the rest of the class.

Development

Possible developments could include discussion and writing on distortion of information, examining bias and looking at the particular slants of newspapers in this country.

Age 14–16 years.

Time A lesson.

N.B. The teacher must not let any member of the acting group be questioned by reporters, nor let anyone else interfere.

Mission survival

Aim

To encourage each pupil to speak persuasively to others in the group.

Requirements   None.

Method

Relate the following situation to the class:

'A rocket is being launched into Earth's orbit to avoid a nuclear holocaust. Six people will be selected to go in the rocket, according to the contribution that each could make to recreating a community of survivors when the rocket returns to earth. What claim do you have to be one of the six?'

Each member of the class must think about their personality and skills, considering their strengths and weaknesses, and choose for themselves a skill, probably fictitious, that they can argue for, e.g.: builder, engineer, doctor, etc.

ROUND ONE   Ask the class to form six groups. The groups are given 10 minutes for each pupil to present their individual case, and for each group to vote for the most persuasive speech.

ROUND TWO   The one person from each group already voted for comes forward to the front of the class to present the skill they have chosen and their suitability for being considered. The rest of the class can then argue their compatibility, and the six formulate their plan of concerted action.

Age   14–18 years.

Time   A lesson.

NARRATIVE FLUENCY

Story game

Aim

To create a co-operative class story without writing it down. A traditional game which also reinforces the difference between a phrase and a sentence.

Requirements   None.

Method

STAGE ONE   Each pupil in turn adds a word to a story. The teacher might choose a theme to start with, or ask a pupil to do so. Keep the story fairly short.

STAGE TWO   Each pupil in turn adds a phrase.

STAGE THREE   Each pupil must add a complete sentence,

e.g.: As the door suddenly swung open there, standing in the darkened porch, was a green dragon, snorting flames... etc.

Age   9–12 years, including slow learners.

Time   15–20 minutes.

N.B. This game works well in conjunction with teaching actual narrative technique.

True or false

Aim

To encourage story-telling technique which is good for confidence-building and helpful for story-writing – fact and fiction. It particularly encourages discrimination in the audience.

Requirements   None.

Method

To begin with, each pupil should think of a factual statement and a fictitious statement about themselves to relate to the rest of the class, who have to guess which is which.

The teacher could start by announcing his or her own statements to the class. Building on this, each pupil then thinks of one true story and one false story to tell the rest of the class.

Again the class attempts to discriminate. This continues until everyone has had a turn at telling their stories.

Age   9–12 years, including slow learners.

Time   A lesson.

Imagine

Aim

To loosen inhibitions and develop the imagination to create stories from ideas contributed by other members of the class.

Requirements   Paper and pen for each pupil.

Method

Ask for four volunteers who come to the front of the class. These four are each asked to close their eyes for a minute and then describe to the class:

  a character
  a place
  a time in history
  the weather conditions.

The class listens to their ideas and then everyone is given five minutes to write a short passage which includes the ideas they have remembered. The class is stopped at the end of five minutes and volunteers read their passages out to the rest of the class.

It is always surprising how many different ideas spring from the same source.

Age   9-12 years, including slow learners.

Time   About twenty minutes.

Innuendo

Aim   To practise directed dialogue in front of a class.

Requirements   None.

Method

Divide the class into pairs. Each pair decides on a topic or subject they are going to discuss. They can also adopt characters, e.g. two telephone engineers discussing the installation of a new telephone.

Each pair takes it in turns to go out to the front of the class to discuss their subject, but they must not mention what it is,

e.g.:   'A': 'Did they choose the Mickey Mouse one in the end?'
'B': 'No, it was too expensive; they went for the digital.'
'A': 'They come in a good range of colours, don't they?'
'B': 'Yeah, they want the blue to go with the curtains.'
'A': 'Is it going on the wall?'
'B': 'No, they can take it where they like; I'm fitting jacks everywhere.'

As the rest of the class listen they try to pick up a clue as to the identity of the pair and the object they are discussing. When they think they have guessed correctly, instead of calling out and interrupting the game, they should try to join in the conversation in character until the majority of the class have realised.

Warning   All innuendo carries obvious connotations!

Age   12–14 years.

Time   10–15 minutes.

Alibis

Aim

To encourage oral discussion and increase powers of deduction.
This is a complicated, but very popular, game.

Requirements   None.

Method

The class creates a fictitious crime with a place, time and date
clearly worked out,

e.g.: The till at the local newsagent's was robbed between the hours
of 6 p.m. and 7.30 p.m. on Saturday last.

Two pupils are chosen to leave the classroom to create alibis. They
should be given a limited time, perhaps two minutes.

Meanwhile, back in the classroom, the teacher should discuss
questioning techniques, for example: moving from the general to the
particular; not giving anything away; jotting down discrepancies, etc.

After two minutes, bring in one of the pair for questioning and again
allow only a limited time for this. The second pupil should then be
brought in, while the first is taken out again. There should be no
opportunity for conferring. The same questions should be asked of
the second pupil.

At the end of the questioning, both pupils should be brought into the
classroom together, and the class should then be allowed to point
out the discrepancies, and decide on their guilt or innocence.

Warning

The initial crime detailed by the class may be unsuitable: rape and
murder are favourites.

Age   12–16 years.

Time   A lesson.

Progressive story telling

Aim

To show how selective the memory can be. This can lead into discussion on rumour and gossip very effectively.

Requirements

A short extract or story to be pre-selected by the teacher. One possibility is included below.

Method

Begin with a game of 'Chinese Whispers'. In this, one pupil thinks of a motto, saying or tongue-twister and whispers it to their neighbour who in turn whispers it to their neighbour, all round the class. The last person to receive the whisper says aloud to the class the message they received.

The game proper begins by sending five volunteers out of the class. The teacher then reads the extract or story to the first volunteer and the rest of the class. The second volunteer then comes in and the first volunteer retells the story in as much detail as they can. The second retells it to the third volunteer and so on, until the last volunteer is in the classroom.

The game ends with the final volunteer recounting their version, and then the teacher reads the original extract again for comparison.

Age   13–15 years.

Time   A lesson.

Prince Kano

One summer's day, Prince Kano was walking through a dark wood when unfortunately he lost his way. All the long day he wandered about searching in vain for a path or a landmark he recognised. The sun was already setting when he stumbled, tired and hungry, across a small clearing in the wood which seemed to be lit with yellow sunlight. There, bending over a brazier, was an old charcoal burner wearing a black hood which covered his face. The Prince cried out for joy: 'Old Man! I will give you whatever you ask: just guide me out of this wood and to the place I live!'

The old charcoal burner slowly looked up and drew the hood back from his face. But he had no face. Instead, where his face should have been, there was an empty space. Half dead with fear, the Prince staggered away and wandered through the wood until the break of day. As the sun rose, he found another clearing in the forest. This clearing was larger and filled with dwellings and people, but somehow his soul was chilled. He looked around for some kind of comfort and his search led him to a small and half-deserted church where monks were praying.

'Father', he said to one of the monks, 'I am afraid. I have just seen a terrible thing!'

'What did you see, my son?'

'I saw an old man and his face was like...' And as the Prince began, the monk drew back his hood and seemed to hiss. He pointed to where his face should have been.

'Like this?'

LANGUAGE GAMES

This chapter includes a very wide selection of games, to encourage versatility and agility with words for every possible purpose.

The first group of word games are simple starters, often ideal for slower learners. Like 'Scrabble' or crosswords, they encourage a basic facility with word forms and letter combinations.

The 'spelling' suggestions could easily be extended: these are just some of the more entertaining ways of testing, and diagnosing, pupils' abilities to spell.

The 'vocabulary and dictionary' games lead the pupils far deeper into the usage of different words. We start with practising the use of alphabetical order, and progress through definitions and synonyms into a serious study of slang and the emotive use of particular vocabulary. These games can be used at quite a high level for language analysis.

Under 'grammatical writing', we use the games format to practice some of the basic rules of grammar: parts of speech, syllables and prefixes, transcribing dialogue.

Finally, under 'language for a purpose', we apply some of these lessons learnt to writing concisely, letter-writing and the specialist use of jargon.

1   WORD GAMES

Heads and tails

Aim   To promote agility with words.

Requirements   None.

Method

Give the class a category of names or objects, e.g.: TOWNS.

After the first town has been nominated, each pupil in turn gives the name of another town whose name begins with the last letter of the previous town, without repeating any mentioned before, e.g.:
London; Norwich; Hartlepool; Littlehampton, etc.

Age   9–12 years, including lower ability pupils.

Time   10–20 minutes.

Nine lives

Aim

To encourage pupils to work co-operatively and quickly, creating words and spelling accurately. This simple spelling game is a useful preliminary to other letter games like 'Lexicon', 'Scrabble' or crosswords.

Requirements   A set of 'Scrabble' letters.

Method

Ask the class to pair off. Each pair at a time is asked to come to the front of the class to pick nine letters from the 'Scrabble' bag.

The teacher writes the letters on the blackboard as they are chosen, then every pair in the class is given 30 seconds to attempt to make a word from these nine letters.

SCORING   If a nine-letter word is made then that pair scores nine points; if an eight-letter word is made, that pair scores eight points, and so on. Each pair should keep their own score.

Age   9–12 years, including slow learners.

Time   A lesson.

Bingo

Aim

To develop an ease with words. This is a simple spelling game which could develop into teaching crossword skills.

Requirements

Paper and a pen for each pupil; a set of 'Scrabble' letters in a bag.

Method

STAGE ONE   Write on the board a category of noun, with the number of letters wanted in the word, then see how quickly the pupils can think of an example of the required length,

e.g.:

Category	Letters	Example
town	7	Swindon
food	8	Weetabix
animal	9	crocodile
football team	11	Bristol City

STAGE TWO   Ask the pupils to think of words which interlock with the first word, of the same category, but of one letter less than the first word,

e.g.:

```
        S W I N D O N              C
                  X               H
                  F         W E E T A B I X
                  O               E
                  R               S
                  D               E


                  E               F
                  L               U
        C R O C O D I L E   B R I S T O L   C I T Y
                  P               H
                  H               A
                  A               M
                  N
                  T
```

34

STAGE THREE The pupils then take one of the categories and make six interlocking words of any length,

```
e.g.:      C
           H              R
       W E E T A B I X
           E              B
           S              E
       B R E A D          N
               A          A
               T
               E G G
```

STAGE FOUR Then select and call out one letter at a time from the 'Scrabble' bag. As the letters are called the pupils cross out the appropriate one until all their letters are deleted. The first pupil to lose all his or her letters shouts, 'Bingo!'

Age 9–12 years, especially slow learners.

Time A lesson.

N.B. This is particularly suitable for pupils who have difficulty with letter values.

Words within words

Aim   To facilitate the creating and spelling of simple words.

Requirements
Rough paper and a pen for each pupil: blackboard and chalk for the teacher.

Method
Write a long word on the blackboard and ask the pupils, either alone or in pairs, to see how many words they can make from those letters. The teacher must decide whether to allow three-letter words, plurals, proper nouns, rude words, etc.

Development
CUBE WORDS   This can lead on to 'Cube Words' where the teacher draws a grid as shown, and jumbles a nine-letter word into the grid:

e.g.: APPLIANCE

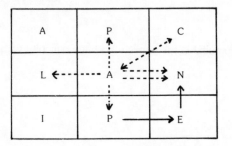

The pupils have to try to make as many words as possible in a sequence within the grid. The sequence is made by tracking from square to adjacent square: see above example.

Age   9–13 years, especially slow learners.

Time   10–15 minutes.

Secret messages

Aim

To provide a game in which pupils create and decipher language or numbers in different symbolic patterns.

Requirements   Paper and a pen for each pupil.

Method

The class is paired off and each pair is asked to write out the letters of the alphabet, A–Z, and the numbers 1–26 underneath. Each pair thinks of a simple message, written in the number code, to send to another pair.

The teacher organises an exchange, and then each pair cracks the code using the number coding.

Development

One of each pair is in prison and writes a letter to their associate outside with a coded message in it. The partner must try to crack the code and decipher the message, then reply using the same code.

Many different codes can be developed and used in games based on espionage, police, radio hams, C.B. radio enthusiasts, flight control, commando units, etc.

Age   9–13 years.

Time   A lesson.

Mnemonics

Aim

To introduce the idea of visual association as a powerful aid to memory.

Requirements   Paper and a pen for each pupil.

Method

Begin by explaining the word 'MNEMONIC'. The pupils should then be asked to give mnemonics that they know, e.g.: Every Good Boy Deserves Favours.

The first method is a simple mnemonic which can be made by giving letters number equivalents, e.g.: A = 1; B = 2; C = 3, etc.

Ask the pupils to make up a mnemonic for their phone number, the school phone number, the doctor's number, etc.

The second method is a rhyming mnemonic. A discussion could develop about the usefulness of these for blind people. This mnemonic can be used to remember items on a list: it uses rhyme and visualisation as aids to memory:

    1 = bun
    2 = shoe
    3 = tree
    4 = door, etc.
(The children can make up the list.)

Itemise a shopping list, e.g.: cheese; soap powder; mince; toilet roll.

Now ask the pupils to visualise the items on the list superimposed on the items in the mnemonic,

e.g.: A bun with cheese filling
    A shoe filled with soap powder
    A tree dripping with mince, etc.

The pupils can be tested at the end of the lesson to see how effective the mnemonic has been. They can also be tested over a period of time: it is amazing how accurate they will be.

Age   9–13 years, especially slow learners.

Time   15 minutes.

Anagrams

Aim

To teach the skills of creating and deciphering anagrams, emphasising the importance of spelling.

Requirements   Paper and a pen for each pupil.

Method

Prepare a list of examples to unscramble, for example on a Christmas theme: 'What's in my stocking?'
1 GURAS SOUME
2 LOTAHOCCE YOMEN
3 ZALEH TUN
4 GINATEERN
5 ALLB TIPON NEP
6 THAB LASTS

The pupils should begin by making anagrams of their own names, after which they can make anagrams of teachers' names. A collection of these anagrams can be made and the pupils asked to unscramble them. (see below for examples and variations.)

Development

The following rhyme may be used to teach what an anagram is:
    Come landlord, fill the flowing POTS
    Until the TOPS run over;
    For on this SPOT
    We needs must STOP
    Until we POST for Dover.

Other words can be found where the words can be rearranged to form a new word, e.g.: HEADS/SHADE/HADES

Sometimes words can be broken down to form other words: it is usual to give the broken-down form and ask the pupils to work out the single word. This skill is useful in solving crossword clues:
    A union sum... UNANIMOUS
    Peg in rich... CIPHERING
    Train time done... DETERMINATION

Letters of a word can just be scrambled to form a jumbled word that has no other meaning, e.g.: RATAFEBKS... Breakfast.

A game can also be played combining clues and anagrams:

CHEAP...A FRUIT = PEACH

A SMALL BOAT...A LARGE SEA = CANOE/OCEAN

GRILLED BREAD...A KIND OF WEASEL = TOAST/STOAT

A VEGETABLE...THE BOTTOM OF A SHIP = LEEK/KEEL

THE MAIN PART OF A CHURCH...WEATHERCOCK = NAVE/VANE

A LARGE BOOK...BIBLICAL SPECK OF DUST = TOME/MOTE

Age   9–13 years.

Time   15 minutes.

2 SPELLING

Word football

Aim To test pupils' spelling.

Requirements
Blackboard, chalk, boardrubber, a dictionary, vocabulary book or exercise books, for each pupil.

Method
1 Ask each pupil to choose two words they can spell, either from dictionaries, vocabulary books, or from corrected spelling in their exercise books. The pupils should then write these two words down.

2 Divide the class into two teams.

3 Number off each team.

4 Draw a pitch on the blackboard, ruled into strips of 25 yards as below with the ball on the centre line:

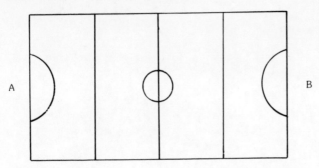

5 Number 1 in Team 'A' asks Number 1 in Team 'B' how to spell their first word. If answered correctly the ball proceeds 25 yards towards A's goal. If the answer is incorrect the ball goes 25 yards towards B's goal.

6 Number 1 on Team 'B' then asks Number 2 on Team 'A' and so on.

7 Goals will be scored and the team with the most goals wins!

Variations

Penalty shots can be awarded by the referee for questioning of decisions, too much noise, bad language, etc.

Age 9–13 years.

Time A lesson.

Fore and aft

Aim   To reinforce spelling and stimulate an interest in words.

Requirements

Paper and a pen for each pupil. A dictionary for consultation over scoring.

Method

Instruct the class to write down as many words as they can think of which begin and end with the same letter, e.g.: BOMB... MADAM... ENVELOPE.

The following rules are good guidelines to make the game more interesting:

1 Only one word can be given for each letter.
2 The pupil who finds the longest word for each letter scores an extra point for it.
3 To break ties in scoring between different words of equal length, the point goes to the word which comes first in the dictionary.

Age

12–14 years. This game is not suitable for children of a dissimilar linguistic ability.

Time   10–20 minutes.

Ghosts (a spelling game)

Aim   To encourage accurate spelling.

Requirements   None.

Method

Each pupil must say a letter in turn round the class. He or she must
have a word in mind when they say the letter, but they may not add
a letter which finishes a word, excepting two- or three-letter words,

e.g.:   The first pupil starts with 'F'; the second pupil adds 'R' (thinking
FRENCH); the third adds 'I' (thinking FRIEND), etc.

If the pupil whose turn it is thinks that the preceding letter was
added without a word in mind, they may challenge. If no word
is given in defence of the challenge, the pupil in the wrong
must forfeit a life. If a word is given, the challenger loses a life.
If a word is ended, a life is lost also. Each pupil begins with
three lives and when a pupil has lost all three lives, he or she
becomes a 'ghost'.

Variations

Traditionally, no one may speak to a ghost. If they do, they become
a ghost too. This may be too complicated for the average
classroom; if so, when all three lives are lost, the person is simply
out.

Age   11–14 years.

Time   10–15 minutes.

3 VOCABULARY AND DICTIONARY GAMES

Scramble

Aim

To practise using alphabetical order, with reference to a dictionary.

Requirements

Two sheets of paper, a pen and a dictionary for each pupil.

Method

Divide the class into pairs or small groups. Ideally each pupil should have a dictionary and each group should be given two pieces of paper.

The teacher instructs the groups to select a particular number of words (10 or 15 for example). These words should be chosen from the dictionary and written in a list down the left-hand side on one of the sheets of paper, in alphabetical order,

e.g.: apple
baboon
coat
daffodil

Each group then folds their piece of paper in half lengthways and in the right-hand column rewrites the list, scrambling the order of the words so that they no longer form an alphabetical list.

e.g.: apple   daffodil
baboon   baboon
coat   apple
daffodil   coat

The group then tears their list down the middle, keeping the alphabetical list. The teacher, or an appointed pupil, collects the scrambled lists and redistributes them. At a given signal, each group now rewrites the new list in alphabetical order on their second piece of paper. The first group to finish is the winner. The completed lists are returned to the original group and checked against the original for accuracy of order and spelling.

Development

This game can be repeated in a varied form. Each group can be allocated one letter and must select words starting with that letter, and repeat the process,

e.g.: cabbage   cinder
      church   cobbler
      cinder   cabbage
      cobbler   church

Age 9-11 years, especially slow learners.

Time This game can take a lesson or be played more quickly.

The alphabet game

Aim To promote agility with vocabulary and grammar.

Requirements

Paper, a pen, and a dictionary for consultation for each pupil.

Method

Ask the class to write a sentence, a paragraph or even a short story, consisting of 26 words beginning with successive letters of the alphabet. Hyphenated words may, but need not, count as one. It can actually be done in one sentence.

e.g.: A brilliant Cockney doctor emerged from Gynaecology, having incautiously just knocked long-suffering matron's neurologist out – protesting (quite rightly so) that untrained veterinarians wouldn't've X-rayed your zygoma.

Age

12–16 years. (This game can be played at all levels of ability.)

Time 10–20 minutes.

Definitions

Aim

To ensure that pupils can write clearly, unambiguously and concisely; and to promote an interest in the meaning of words and the use of the dictionary.

Requirements

A dictionary for each pupil if possible; list of words for defining. This list should depend upon the nature of the class participating in the game. A list of nouns like LADDER, PAPER, TELEPHONE, PRUNE, for example, would be appropriate for a young class.

A list containing more abstract ideas would be more taxing for older or more able pupils: PAIN, ANGER, GRIEF, COLOUR.

Method

STAGE ONE Each pupil is privately given a different word to define. It might be useful to start by using one common example which the pupils can all examine in their dictionaries.

In turn, each pupil reads out their definition, and the other members of the class write down what they think the word is. The dictionary definitions can also be found and a comparison made.

STAGE TWO Each pupil can be asked to write a definition of the same word and then each in turn reads their definition out. The best can be selected and compared with the definition given in the dictionary.

Age

11–14 years. This game can be played with a wide range of age and ability groups, but the material chosen must be appropriate to the particular group.

Time A lesson.

N.B. The second method is more effective with older pupils and with the more abstract words.

What's my word?

Aim   To use dictionary definitions, and to extend vocabulary.

Requirements   Dictionary; blackboard and chalk for scoring.

Method

Divide the class into two teams, and number the members of each team.

Number 1 from Team A comes to the front of the class and selects a word from the dictionary. They read the brief definition of meaning aloud to both teams.

Anyone who guesses the word from the definition alone, from either team, may put their hand up. The first hand up may attempt to answer and if they are correct, their team receives five points.

If they are incorrect, then the first clue is given, i.e. the first letter of the word. The first hand up from either team may guess again for four points.

If the guess is still wrong, the second clue (the second letter) is given, and so on,

e.g.:   The definition given is: 'a young female horse'. There are no takers. The first clue is given: it starts with 'f'. 'Foal' is suggested: it is incorrect. The second clue is given: 'f-i'. 'Filly' is guessed, for a score of three points.

Age   11–16 years.

Time   A lesson.

N.B. It might be useful to have a second dictionary to hand to speed the game up.

Call my bluff

Aim

To increase vocabulary and to familiarise the pupils with the use of a dictionary.

Requirements

Dictionary, paper and a pen for each pupil; blackboard and chalk.

Method

Each pupil should find a difficult word in the dictionary and write down the definition. They then make up two false definitions of the word.

They should be able to state what kind of word it is, i.e. noun, verb, adjective, etc. and be reminded that each of the three definitions should describe the same part of speech as the dictionary definition.

The class should be divided into two teams, A and B, and the pupils in each team should number off. Number 1 of Team A puts their word to Number 1 of Team B; Number 1 of Team B to Number 2 of Team A, etc.

The first pupil writes their word on the blackboard, and then gives three definitions. Their opposite number must choose one of the definitions. If they make the correct choice, they score a point for their team.

Extension

The teacher should go through the words at the end of the lesson to see how many correct definitions can be remembered. It is also a good game for pronunciation practice.

Warning

There will always be some words that everyone else has heard of. This can be avoided if the teacher checks the words as they are selected, and before the definitions are made up.

Age   13–15 years.

Time   A lesson.

N.B. This game is modified from the original first game so that each pupil participates, rather than a select few.

Synonyms

Aim

To practise finding synonyms, thereby extending pupils' vocabulary.

Requirements

A thesaurus for when pupils run out of their own synonyms.

Method

The class is divided into two teams, and the members of each team are numbered, e.g. 1 to 15. Give team A a word from the list below or from a thesaurus,

e.g.: fat. All the numbers from 1–15 have to try to contribute a synonym of that word in turn, e.g.: 1 – stout; 2 – plump; 3 – gross, etc.

The team scores a point for each new synonym given. Those who cannot think of one have to pass, but can have 'free time' at the end for extra words not thought of in the course of the game.

Team B is then given a different word and the game is repeated.

Warning

On alternate rounds for each team start with number 15 instead of number 1, as the game obviously becomes more difficult towards the end.

Age   11–13 years.

Time   A lesson.

Useful words to start with

gain	straight	just	flourish
crowd	judge	break	exercise
sympathy	drop	correct	fine

Same or different

Aim   To practise finding synonyms and antonyms.

Requirements   Paper and a pen for each pupil.

Method

First explain what synonyms and antonyms are. The class is then divided into pairs.

STAGE ONE   Each pair is given a word from the list below, and writes down a synonym and an antonym for the word.

STAGE TWO   Each pair takes it in turn to read out both the synonym and the antonym while the rest of the class try to guess what the original word is. The teacher should be lenient towards plausible suggestions, even if they are not the word which the pair is working from.

Allow the class to judge how many of the guesses are plausible.

Age   14–16 years.

Time   A lesson.

Key words

active	fair	modesty
anxious	freedom	persuade
assist	generous	random
calm	gradual	rapid
careful	happy	safe
common	hate	secretive
complex	hesitant	sensitive
condemn	immediate	shy
descent	incredible	
difficult	intelligent	

Good, bad and better

Aim

To encourage pupils to find synonyms for over-worked words.

Requirements   Paper and a pen for each pupil.

Method

Ask the pupils to suggest which are the most over-worked words in their writing. What extra effect do they achieve with more unusual vocabulary?

Now set up the game. In pairs, the pupils see how many synonyms they can find for words like 'said', 'got', 'went', etc. If pupils really work through all the possible alternatives for each word, this can turn into an extended dictionary game.

End with a piece of written work in which the key words are banned, and the new lists are put into use.

Age   9–13 years.

Time   A lesson.

Malapropisms

Aim

To teach the meaning of the term 'malapropism' and to increase vocabulary and word-awareness.

Requirements

The teacher prepares a list of malapropisms (see below). Dictionaries might be useful.

Method

Explain the meaning of the word 'malapropism' and give a list of examples. The pupils should be asked to spot the malapropism and substitute the correct word,

e.g.: Birds rotate in winter.
Hedgehogs moderate when it is cold.
Take a spoonful of fixative for constipation.
Swab! Biceps! Nurse!

When the pupils have completed the examples, they can make up their own malapropisms.

Since the point of a malapropism must be its approximation to another word in the person's vocabulary, this game will actually cover a very wide range of vocabulary. The pupils must be able to justify each malapropism by first substituting the correct word of similar sound, and then demonstrating their understanding of the misused word by using it in its correct context.

Age 11–13 years.

Time A lesson.

Slang is for real

Aim

To make pupils realise that language is a constantly changing phenomenon.

Requirements

Dictionary, paper and pen for each pupil. (If the teacher wishes to use further examples, use a dictionary of slang.)

Method

Explain that slang exists for a variety of reasons, such as a comic substitute for the usual form,

e.g.: for dying or death: snuffing it; pushing up the daisies; kicking the bucket; popping off. Or to provide a new word for a new idea, or to adapt on existing word or phrase, e.g.: punk; New Wave; straights; wheelies.

Pupils are asked to make their own lists of current words or expressions. This collection should include slang terms and colloquialisms. If the pupils find it difficult to start, the teacher can direct them towards music, clothes, expressions of praise or insult, crazes, etc.

The pupils should then be asked to define what the terms mean, writing them out as serious dictionary definitions. In this way they will also learn the conventions of dictionary terminology.

Age   9–15 years.

Time

This collection is best made over a period of time. Pupils can add to their collections in spare minutes. Results can be collated and brought together at any suitable time.

Rabbit and pork – rhyming talk

Aim

To make pupils aware of an amusing and inventive type of slang.

Requirements   Paper and pen for each pupil.

Method

Give the pupils examples of rhyming slang (see below).

STAGE ONE   Ask the pupils to form pairs and make up their own rhyming slang.

STAGE TWO   When they have thought up some examples, they can improvise a conversation using their own rhyming slang and act it out in front of the rest of the class, who can listen and try to guess the subject of the conversation.

Age   9–13 years, including slow learners.

Time   A lesson.

Examples

pimple and blotch	Scotch
frog and toad	road
4th July	tie
almond rocks	socks
apple fritter	bitter (ale)
Artful Dodger	lodger
sugar and honey	money

Animal crackers

Aim To awaken pupils to the richness of animal imagery.

Requirements Paper and a pen for each pupil.

Method

STAGE ONE Divide the class into small groups then explain that each group is to collect together words or phrases which are derived from animal behaviour,

e.g.: to rat on someone; slothful; dog in the manger; wolfing it
      down, etc.

A quarter of an hour is the recommended period of time to spend on this. When the groups have finished, a spokesperson from each group reads out their list.

STAGE TWO Each member of the group chooses one of the words or phrases that they particularly liked, and tries to explain in writing the reason why that particular animal has given rise to that metaphor,

e.g.: slothful: meaning slow-moving and lazy. The adjective is
      appropriate because the sloth moves slowly.

Some of the derivations may not be known by the pupils and may not easily be guessed at, but the teacher using a *Brewer's Dictionary of Phrase and Fable* could do some interesting work with the pupils, or they could be taught to use this dictionary as a reference book,

e.g.: a dog in the manger: a mean-spirited individual. The allusion is
      to the fable of the dog who fixed his place in a manger and
      would not allow the ox to come near the hay, but would not
      eat it himself.

Age 11–13 years.

Time A lesson.

Examples

ants in your pants	bear with a sore head	bird-brained
bat out of hell	bee in the bonnet	bitch
batty	bees' knees	braying
bear hug	bird	catty

chick
chicken
chameleon
clawing back
codding
cow
crazy as a coot
crocodile tears
crowing
crow's feet
cocky
crabby
dead as a dodo
doe-eyed
dog-eared
dogged
doggish
dog in the manger
dragon
drunk as a skunk
ducking
fawning
ferreting about
fishy
fly in the ointment
fly on the wall
foxed
foxing
fishing for
   compliments

hair of the dog
happy as a lark
hang-dog
hare-brained
haring about
hawking
hog's wash
horse-play
hung for a sheep as
   a lamb
kidding
kittenish
lark about
laughing like a hyena
leonine
lounge lizard
mole
mother hen
mulish
mutton dressed up
   as lamb
owlish
paper tiger
pigeon-chested
pigeon-toed
pigging about
pig's ear
pig-sick
proud as a
   peacock

puppy fat
rabbiting on
real skunk
shark
shrew
sick as a dog
sing like a nightingale
slippery as an eel
sluggish
snake in the grass
snaking
slothful
sow
stud
swanning about
tiger's eyes
toad
to eat like a horse
vixen
waspish
water off a duck's
   back
weasle
webbed feet
whale of a time
wise as an owl
wolf in sheep's clothing
wolfing it down
worming

Hidden message

Aim

To pick out emotive words in written passages.

Requirements

Stage One: one short newspaper clipping for each pupil. Stage Two: longer newspaper articles or poetry. 'Magic Marker' pens.

Method

STAGE ONE   Ask the pupils to bring newspaper reports to the lesson, particularly emotive reports with a noticeable bias. Each pupil picks out the words which contribute to the newspaper's point of view, e.g.: references to 'standards' of education, or the 'violence' of demonstrations. These are the words which build up the 'hidden message'.

STAGE TWO   Then, the class may go on to repeat the exercise on a longer article or in quite a different medium, such as poetry, again picking out the words which contribute to the emotive effect.

Age   14–16 years.

Time   A lesson-starter for detailed work on the use of language.

4 GRAMMATICAL WRITING

The naming game

Aim   To teach the function of the noun as a naming word.

Requirements

Paper and a pen for each pupil; blackboard and chalk.

Method

STAGE ONE   Explain the function of the noun then ask the class to think of as many nouns as possible, beginning with selected letters of the alphabet.

STAGE TWO   Write up a number of group headings, e.g.: name, fruit, vegetable, tree, mammal, article of clothing, etc.

Again a letter is chosen and each pupil writes down a noun for each category, beginning with the chosen letter. The game can be made competitive by introducing scoring and time limits.

Make sure that any words which do not qualify as nouns are discussed with the class.

Possible developments

The teacher can use this game to make the distinction between proper nouns and common nouns, and the use of the capital letter.

Age   9–13 years, especially slow learners.

Time   15–35 minutes.

Collective nouns

Aim

To teach collective nouns and to provide the stimulus for pupils to invent their own collective nouns.

Requirements   None.

Method

Write some examples on the board to teach the idea of a collective noun,

e.g. a gaggle of geese.
      a pride of lions.
      a litter of puppies.

The teacher can then proceed to give the pupils nouns and ask them to add the appropriate collective idea,

e.g.: a..................of bees.
      a..................of aircraft.
      a..................of buffalo.

The pupils can then be introduced to the idea of inventing their own collective nouns. Dylan Thomas's examples can be used to introduce the idea: 'a lark of boys'; 'a giggle of girls'; 'a silent hullabaloo of balloons'.

The pupils can be given nouns or they can use their own ideas. The results can be illustrated and displayed.

Age   11–13 years.

Time   About 15 minutes.

Adverbs – in the manner of the word

Aim

To introduce a light-hearted approach to the function of the adverb.

Requirements   None.

Method

Begin by explaining what an adverb is: that it tells us something more about the verb in terms of how, when or where the action takes place.

When the class understands the adverb, each pupil is asked to pick an adverb but to keep the choice secret. One volunteer is asked to come to the front of the class. The rest of the class must think of things that the volunteer can be asked to perform. The tasks must be performed in the manner of the adverb they have chosen,

e.g.: The pupil might have chosen 'clumsily', and he or she might be asked to open a window or put a book on to the teacher's desk in the manner of this word.

When the adverb is correctly guessed, another pupil may have a turn at acting their adverb.

Age   9–13 years and slow learners.

Time   10–15 minutes.

Grammatical consequences

Aim   To practise the parts of speech.

Requirements   A strip of paper and a pen for each pupil.

Method

Begin by writing a model like this on the board:

The
green   (adjective)
elephant (noun)
ate   (verb)
the
aged   (adjective)
judge   (noun)

The teacher should make sure the class are familiar with these parts of speech, then distribute strips of paper. Each pupil first writes an adjective, then folds it over and passes it to the next pupil. They then write a noun, fold it over and pass the paper on, until the sentence has been completed.

Each paper is passed on for the last time and then opened. The pupil is allowed to change the tense of the verb and add pronouns or small words to improve the result, and the funniest or most original can be judged. More complex sentences can be suggested for the model when the class are ready to progress.

Age   11–13 years.

Time   A lesson.

Dictation with a difference

Aim   To consolidate the understanding of parts of speech.

Requirements   Paper and a pen for each pupil.

Method

When a class has been taught the parts of speech, the teacher can make up a dictation leaving blanks for the pupils to fill in, but telling them what kind of words to choose,

e.g.: Lady Blanket ......(verb), ...(adverb). She ......(verb) at her ......(noun).
'Pass the ......(noun)', she ......(verb).

The results are usually quite amusing, especially to the pupils.

Warning

This game can be very amusing and constructive but can also be abused. The teacher should penalise unhelpful contributions.

Age   11–13 years.

Time   15 minutes.

Pyramids

Aim

To reinforce pupils' understanding of syllables.

Requirements   Paper and a pen for each pupil; dictionaries.

Method

First, explain or revise the division of words into syllables. The object of the game is then to make up a pyramid of words with a one-syllable word at the top of the pyramid, a two-syllable word beneath it, a three-syllable one, and so on. These can be grouped by subject or initial letter. Credit should be given for the highest pyramid.

e.g.:

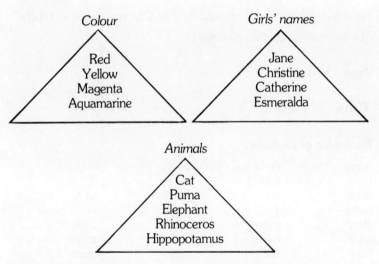

The finished products make good display material and can be illustrated imaginatively.

Age   9–11 years.

Time   15 minutes.

Prefixes

Aim

To unravel meanings through understanding that many words in our language are compounds of a prefix and a stem.

Requirements

Dictionaries, paper, a pen and a teacher's list of common prefixes (see below).

Method

The class is divided into pairs and each pair is given a prefix by the teacher. Firstly, each pair must find the meaning of the prefix. Then, each pair must make a list of words which begin with that prefix and their meanings,

e.g.: TRI = three: tripod; triangle; tricycle; (but not of course tripe!).

The lists can be usefully displayed.

Age   12–14 years.

Time   A lesson.

Examples of prefixes

aero	ambi	anti	audio
com	con	de	di
cent	dis	electro	ex
extra	il	im	in
inter	intro	micro	milli
mini	mis	mono	multi
non	off	out	over
per	photo	post	pre
pro	radio	re	semi
stereo	sub	suc	suf
sum	super	sur	tele
trans	un	uni	well

Eavesdroppers

Aim

To practise how to turn direct speech into reported speech within an imaginative context. The game also exercises memory.

Requirements

Paper and a pen for each pupil, with situation cards (see below).

Method

The pupils volunteer in pairs to come to the front of the class and select a situation. They decide upon their roles and improvise the situation given on the card.

The rest of the class are eavesdropping on what occurs and when the acting has finished the class attempts to write about what they overheard using direct speech first. Then, for 'newspaper' purposes, they convert it into reported speech. Alternatively, half the class can record the dialogue in direct and half in reported speech, so that the contrasting effects can be compared.

Warning

It is advisable for the teacher to set a time-limit on the improvisations: two minutes is suggested: also to have the class ready to write with paper and pens so there is minimal disruption between the improvisations and the exercise of writing.

Age   11–13 years.

Time   10–20 minutes.

Possible situations

1 Two people on a bus complaining about youth today.
2 Two prisoners discussing plans for a break-out.
3 A disagreement between a ticket collector and a passenger who has lost his ticket.
4 An argument between two motorists, both of whom backed into the same parking place.

5 An experienced policeman/woman taking a raw recruit on the beat.

6 A salesperson trying to sell an unusual article to a talkative householder.

7 An undiscovered singer trying to interest an influential disc jockey.

8 A fortune-teller reading a tourist's palm.

9 An irate walker complaining to a farmer about the aggressive bull in his field.

10 Two neighbours discussing the arrival of a newcomer to the district.

5 LANGUAGE FOR A PURPOSE

Teleletters

Aim

To practise the skills of writing economically, and to use the skills of listening and writing in a practical situation.

Requirements   Paper and a pen for each pupil.

Method

Each pupil is given a piece of paper and asked to make up and write down a situation requiring the sending of a teleletter,

e.g.: Your great aunt Maud has fallen down the stairs and broken her leg.

Your sister has had triplets.

Your uncle will arrive at the airport tomorrow and will want someone to meet him.

The situations are collected up and redistributed. Each pupil, having picked out a situation, must write a teleletter in rough form to communicate that information. The pupils should be reminded that there is generally a fixed rate for 50 words so the letter should not exceed that length.

The class then divides into pairs. In turns, one of the pair will dictate their teleletter while the other role-plays the telephonist and takes down the letter, spelling and punctuating it carefully. The roles are then changed over and finally the teleletters are checked for accuracy.

Age   9–13 years.

Time   A lesson.

Shop window

Aim

To familiarise pupils with the procedure and techniques required in placing and answering an advertisement.

Requirements

Newspaper. Pen and paper for each pupil. The rates per word should be written on the board,

e.g.: 1 ordinary word... 20p
1 large type word... 35p

Method

Ask the class to imagine an item that they would like to sell. Each pupil writes a very detailed description of the object on a piece of paper. The pieces are folded up and collected in a hat, and then redistributed. Each pupil then reads the description of the object and pares it down to the essentials to make a suitable advertisement for the local paper.

These advertisements are then placed back in the hat and redistributed again. Each pupil then costs the advertisement he or she recieves, and rates its effectiveness as selling copy.

Age 9–14 years.

Time A lesson.

Complaints

Aim   To teach the layout of formal letter-writing.

Requirements   Paper and a pen for each pupil.

Method

Divide the class into pairs and ask each pair to choose the name of a firm and then ask them to create a fictitious address,

e.g.: Baps the Bakers
30 High Street
Little Puckleham.

Write a list of all the firms and their addresses on the board and allocate a partner to each. Each firm must write a letter of complaint to the firm they have been linked with, following the simple format which the teacher can display on the board.

The teacher should act as the postman and deliver the letters once they have been written. The firm complained to should write a letter to answer the complaint.

Variations

If there are delays, letters of complaint can be written to any other firm on the board.

Impolite letters can be dealt with by the postman.

Age   11–12 years.

Time   A lesson.

Speed-writing

Aim

To loosen the inhibited writer and give the pupils the opportunity to discover for themselves that there is more to writing than quantity.

Requirements   Paper and a pen for each pupil.

Method

ROUND ONE   First, have a competition to see which pupil can write the most in a minute. The teacher chooses a subject and the pupils are told they must write as much as they can on the subject within the minute, not concerning themselves with how it is written. When the teacher declares the subject, e.g. BALLOONS, the class begin to write.

The teacher times a minute, then stops the class and asks each pupil to count the number of words written, and to write this total clearly on their papers.

ROUND TWO   This can follow with each pupil trying to better their own score.

The teacher can then ask the pupils to work out how many words they could write in their allotted homework time if they can write the number of words counted in the number of minutes given! The pupils will sense the injustice of this and immediately suggest what other things have to be taken into account, e.g. punctuation, presentation, selection, organisation of ideas, etc.

Variations

The game can continue with each pupil being asked to take one of their pieces and prune it, punctuate it, write it neatly and then compare the value of the two pieces.

Age   12–14 years.

Time   Lesson starter.

N.B. This game can really be played once only with any one group.

Substitute

Aim   To introduce editing skills.

Requirements   Paper and a pen for each pupil.

Method

Ask the class to work in pairs. Each pupil either produces a piece of previous written work, or writes one especially for this exercise.

When everyone is ready they exchange articles with their partners, who will read the work carefully and asterisk weak words or correct inaccuracies, e.g.: nice, good, sad, went, said, etc.

The work is then given back to the original owners and the amendments are discussed.

Note that this exercise should be done in a spirit of supportive collaboration, not vindictiveness!

Age   12-16 years: can be interpreted at different levels.

Time   A lesson.

Jargon

Aim

To help pupils to understand the role of jargon in specialist and non-specialist subjects.

Requirements

Paper and a pen for each pupil; dictionaries; thesaurus; examples of jargon in use (see below for examples).

Method

Begin by explaining the different effects of jargon: that it acts as a form of shorthand for specialist audiences, but is a barrier, whether deliberate or unconscious, to lay audiences.

The class should then divide into pairs and think up a simple idea or activity which is sometimes dressed up in 'jargonese',

e.g.: Emptying a dustbin: the act of making vacant a receptacle for the containment of odorous and excess matter.

One pupil from each pair should read out the jargon and the rest of the class guesses what the simple activity is. Why do officials sometimes exaggerate their language in such cases? Let the class discuss.

Extension

The teacher can easily find examples of jargon at work, in political speeches, newspaper articles, magazines, advertisements, sporting reviews, etc. Examples can be given out to the class and the pupils can be asked to underline the jargon and rewrite the underlying ideas. (see Gowers, *Plain Words*.)

Age   14–16 years.

Time   A lesson. The idea can be extended.

Examples of specialist jargon

'A variety of locos have been used for this service, but nearly all have been based on the Triang Big Train 0–4–0 chassis which uses 4 HP11 cells and which is available under the Novo marque in either the "Ruston" or "Sammy the Shunter" guise...'

(*Model Railways*)

'A sector of ore milling which has generated much interest, development and debate in recent years has been autogenous grinding, either full or partial. In the latter method, usually referred to as semi-autogenous, steel balls are used as the grinding media in fully autogenous mills...'

(*Mining Magazine*)

'The same methods that Ashland uses to determine whether assets should be in equities or money-market certificates are applied on the microlevel for the purpose of selecting particular stocks out of their universe of 800. If, based on Ashland's criteria, a stock is more than 40% undervalued, it is considered a "buy". Between 40% under valuation and equal value, it is in a "hold" category, and when selling at a premium, the stock is considered a "sell".'

(*Stockbroking Journal*)

STIMULUS TO WRITING

This section of the book is designed to help the pupils who are deterred by being given a blank piece of paper and a title, and being told 'now go away and write'. It is not only the pupils with real writing difficulties who need this help; any pupil will produce better work, often surprisingly better work, when their writing tasks are focused by audience, purpose and style.

The 'descriptive' games encourage pupils to develop more precision and imagination in their descriptive writing.

The 'poetry' games should develop more knowledge and understanding of poetic form, and they can easily be extended into different genres of poetic writing: children happily take to writing haikus, ballads, sonnets, when given definitions and examples of the different forms.

The suggestions for 'imaginative writing' could be endless; we have simply tried to set up situations which should motivate pupils to write extended narrative. The most successful by far is always 'Titanic', with its combination of emphatic demands in an authentic historical setting. This situation could be replicated with any topical news items involving survival, e.g. Evacuation from Three Mile Island.

Finally, the 'functional writing' section sharpens up the particular skills needed to particular audiences in particular mediums, e.g. writing instructions, writing for newspapers and brochures.

1   DESCRIPTIVE

What am I?

Aim

To be able to describe an object clearly from imagination.

Requirements   Paper and a pen for each pupil.

Method

Take a category of items, such as fruit or vegetables. Ask each pupil to describe on paper one object they have chosen, with reference to the size, the texture, smell, colour and shape, but being careful NOT to mention what the object is.

Each pupil reads their description in turn, ending with the words, 'What am I?', and the rest of the class guesses.

Age   9–12 years.

Time

This can take as much time as the teacher deems appropriate to the needs of the class.

Hide and seek

Aim

To encourage pupils to describe places clearly, thinking about conveying atmosphere through the five senses.

Requirements   Paper and a pen for each pupil.

Method

Each pupil must choose a hiding place; a restriction may be the location to the school, the neighbourhood, or a place that is possible.

Each describes the place where they are hiding, taking care to think of the exact conditions, for example, what they can feel – under foot, beside them, what they are sitting on, etc. They should also think very carefully about smell, heat, cold, etc. Each person must be careful NOT to mention where they are but must leave the reader to guess, ending with the words: 'Where am I hiding?'.

Age   9–12 years, including slow learners.

Time   A lesson.

Sale of the century

Aim

To encourage pupils to describe objects carefully from observation.

Requirements

The pupils should be asked in advance to bring in an object which is as bizarre as they can find.

Method

Each pupil should write a detailed description of their object, concentrating on the relationship between appearance and function.

The teacher can add the idea that the pupils are all archaeologists of the twenty-first century, or invaders from another planet, and these are the things they find, giving clues as to how people lived in the twentieth century.

Either the pupils read their reports aloud in turn, with the rest of the class guessing what is being described; or the descriptions can be exchanged, and the new readers guess the objects. They can then exchange objects and try a further description.

Age   11–13 years.

Time   A lesson.

Nature trail

Aim

To help pupils to use detail and specific example in descriptive writing. The pupils with more local knowledge will be encouraged to share it with those who know less.

Requirements

Paper and a pen for each pupil; blackboard and chalk.

Method

The teacher writes a number of categories of nature on the board, e.g.: flowers; trees; birds; clouds; colours.

The class should then write down as many specific examples of these as they can in an allotted period of time. Some pupils will, of course, know many more names for some categories than for others. These lists should be discussed and a collective list assembled so that the pupils can use more specific detail in descriptive writing.

Try it out immediately with a piece of detailed description of the river bank, the wood in autumn, etc. The same exercise can, of course, be carried out on urban description, or more specific locations like stations, airports, hypermarkets, etc.

Age   11-14 years.

Time   A lesson.

If...

Aim

To encourage pupils to be perceptive about character and express those perceptions in an imaginative way.

Requirements   Paper and a pen for each pupil.

Method

The class choose a well-known personality. The teacher then writes a list of categories on the board (see below). The class suggest appropriate comparisons for completing the character study (see example).

The pupils should then divide into pairs and try completing character studies of each other using the same format.

Warning

The pupils should be allowed to form their own partnerships, but the teacher should be aware that opportunities for unkindness and silliness do present themselves.

Age   11-13 years.

Time   20 minutes.

Example:

Kenny Everett.
If he were a flower he would be a marigold.
If he were a fruit... banana
                vegetable... spinach
                piece of furniture... deckchair
                colour... pink
                animal... monkey
                type of weather... sunny
                bird... robin
                type of food... spaghetti
                drink... cherryade
                musical instrument... piccolo.

Market place

Aim

To direct the pupils' attention to sensory perception and encourage them to write in detail, capturing the essence of the subject matter.

Requirements   Stall-holders' cards (see the list below).

Method

The teacher writes a list of the five senses on the board: *taste*, *touch*, *sound*, *smell* and *sight*. Make the point that good atmospheric descriptive writing appeals to our senses and declare that the aim of the game is to build up atmosphere in description through the use of unusual detail.

PART ONE: ORAL   Describe the market place to the class. Each member of the class is asked to think of a word, phrase or sentence which describes a facet of the market place and which appeals to one of the five senses (see below).

(The first few suggestions will probably be clichéd but the later contributions are likely to be progressively more interesting and original. If this pattern of response emerges help the class to discriminate between the original and the clichéd contribution.)

PART TWO: WRITTEN   Each pupil is given a stall-holders' card. They have to describe their part in the market, concentrating on appealing to the five senses. The class may arrange the images and ideas as they wish and present their finished work either as a prose paragraph or as a poem.

Age   12–14 years.

Time   A lesson.

Stalls

flowers	bedding
fruit and vegetables	watches
fabrics	car accessories
meat	records and cassettes
fish	jeans
china	jewellery

electrical appliances	rugs and carpets
shoes	wholefoods
leather and fur coats	hot dogs
toys	ice creams
sweets	hot chestnuts
biscuits and cakes	etc.

Examples

Sight: a child pulling at a mother's shopping bag.

Smell: damp paper bags.

Touch: greasy bank notes changing hands.

Sound: 'In the shops at £10. Yours for only £2!'

Taste: a sweet rubbery hot dog splattered with mustard and sauce.

2 POETIC

Riddles

Aim

To demonstrate examples of different kinds of riddle, and encourage the pupils to write their own.

Requirements   Paper and a pen for each pupil.

Method

Either read out these examples to the class or, preferably, invite the pupils to bring their own. The main genres you could attempt to cover are as follows:

1 What's old and shakes at the bottom of the sea?
  A nervous wreck.

2 Why did the coal scuttle?
  Because it saw the kitchen sink.

3 What is the difference between a lazy schoolboy and a fisherman?
  One hates his books and the other baits his hooks.

4 My first is in bread sauce but not in the gravy;
  My second's in straight lines but not found in wavy;
  My third is in pumpkin but not in the pie;
  My fourth is in full-up but not in the sigh;
  My fifth is in cake-frill but not in the cake;
  My sixth is in ice but not on the lake;
  My seventh's in candle but not in the wick;
  My eighth's found in groaning but not found in sick.
  What am I?

5 Awoke and stretched in all the glories
  lofted on sinewy air. Clipped out
  beak-shaped cries and skinned the mist
  from the morning... (*Birds*)

                          (May Swenson, *Junior Voices*)

After examining these forms and solving the examples, the pupils can be asked to choose one of the forms and make up their own riddle. The riddles can be written up and put up round the classroom and the pupils can attempt to solve as many as possible in the time that can be allowed..

Age 9–14 years.

Time A whole lesson.

Alliteration

Aim

To teach the meaning of this device and to experiment with its effect in writing.

Requirements   Paper and a pen for each pupil.

Method

After discussing the meaning of the word 'alliteration' the teacher can illustrate its use. One area where alliteration can be effectively used is in advertising.

Each pupil picks a letter and thinks of a product that begins with that letter, then writes an alliterative piece extolling the virtues of the product,

e.g.: The pupil picks the letter 'P'.
'Pork Pies! A Product without Parallel... so Perfect for Parties... Produced from Prime Plump, Pink Pigs!'

Then move the pupils on to using alliteration in poetic writing, choosing the appropriate letter for the sound to be conveyed.

Age   9–13 years, including slow learners.

Time   A lesson or part of a lesson, at the teacher's discretion.

Paperchain

Aim

To use the simple idea of associating ideas to expand into more considered poetic writing. This game can be developed from the word-association game (Blue Moon Crackers) in the Oral Section.

Requirements   Paper and a pen for each pupil.

Method

Each pupil chooses a colour, a mood, an element, a season, etc. They then write the chosen word at the top of their paper. The pupils then proceed to write a list of associations, simple single words or extended ideas.

When pupils have collected together the words associated in their minds with the initial word, they can then be encouraged to arrange their ideas, discarding those that do not appear to be helpful or well-expressed, and thus making up a poem on that original theme,

e.g.: ELEMENT
    Water
    Smooth and false as glass
    Dark as a dream
    White spume
    False dissembler
    Luring enticing
    Drowning wrecking
       (Paul Jeffries, aged 12½)

The poems can be illustrated with collage work and attractively displayed.

Age   9–14 years.

Time   A lesson.

Rhyming couplets

Aim

To teach easy scanning, concentrating on stressed and unstressed syllables.

Requirements   Paper and a pen for each pupil.

Method

It is necessary to explain rhyme pattern and metre before beginning the game. This can be done by writing a couplet on the board and explaining the stress pattern of the lines,

e.g.: As I was walking down the street,
I met a man with two left feet.

Each pupil begins by writing one line in the same metre as that given in the example. When every pupil is ready they all pass their pieces of paper to the person on their right, who writes the second line. Line two must scan and rhyme.

When this line is written, the child must fold back the first line so that only the line just written is visible. When every member is ready the papers are passed on again, for the third line to be written. This line must scan but should not rhyme.

The second line must then be folded back so that only the last line is visible. The papers are passed on again. The fourth line must rhyme and scan.

The process is repeated until an eighth line has been written and the poem has been finished, the page is folded over and passed on for the last time. The final recipients open them and may make minor alterations. The poems are then read out by the pupils or by the teacher.

Possible developments

To look at rhyme and metre in poetry, e.g. the works of Linton Kwesi Johnson, John Cooper Clarke, Bob Dylan, etc.

Age   13–16+ years.

Time   A lesson.

N.B. Some pupils may have difficulties with rhyme and metre; the teacher should try to identify these pupils and use the game as a way of working collectively on the weaker lines.

Cloze poems

Aim

To help pupils to think about the precise choice of words in poetic writing.

Requirements

A chosen poem, such as the example opposite:

Method

Write the poem on the blackboard, and ask the class to copy it down. Various words should be blanked out; the words chosen can be fairly random, but they should be the ones which will provoke the liveliest discussion – e.g. those marked in italics.

Ask the class to speculate on which word the poet would have chosen to use at each point. Emphasise that there is not a right or wrong choice, but they should use the clues of context, rhyme and metre where possible to influence their suggestions.

Finally show the class the full poem, and again discuss the poet's chosen words with relation to the pupils' anticipations.

Age   13–16 years.

Time   Can take a whole lesson.

The Secret in the Cat

I took my cat apart
to see what made him purr.
Like an electric clock
or like the *snore*

of a warming kettle,
something fizzled and sizzled in him
Was he a soft car,
the engine bubbling sound?

Was there a wire beneath his fur,
or humming *throttle*?
I undid his throat.
Within was no stir.

I opened up his chest
as though it were a *door*:
no whisk or rattle there.
I lifted off his skull:

no hiss or murmur.
I halved his little belly
but found no gear,
no cause for static.

So I replaced his lid
laced his little gut.
His heart into his vest I slid
and buttoned up his throat.

His tail rose to a rod
and beckoned to the air.
some *voltage* made him vibrate
warmer than before.

Whiskers and a tail:
perhaps they caught
some radar code
emitted as a pip, a dot-and-dash

of woollen sound.
My cat a kind of tuning fork? –
amplifier? – *telegraph*? –
doing secret signal work?

His eyes elliptic tubes:
There's a message in his stare.
I stroke him
but cannot find the dial.

(May Swenson)

Sequencing

Aim

To provide pupils with the opportunity to discover for themselves the way in which a poem works. By presenting the pupils with a fragmented poem, they can build it up for themselves and so find out about the structure of the poem, and the most effective arrangement of words.

Requirements

The teacher will need to write out a poem, or several poems, on card, and then cut it/them into lines or stanzas, keeping each poem in a separate envelope.

Method

Begin by dividing the class into small groups. Give each group a poem cut up into lines. Each group is then asked to arrange the lines into the form of a poem.

The group, through discussion, should discover the metric pattern and the rhyme scheme of the poem. They should also be able to focus on the placing of words and the relationship between the form and the content.

At the end of the allotted time, ask the group to compare their arrangement with the original version. Time should be allowed for each group to discuss any differences that might have occurred.

This game can be played with the youngest pupils up to and including the oldest and most academic, but the material chosen should suit the particular group. John Masefield's 'Sea-Fever' or William Blake's 'Tyger, Tyger' work well with fourth-year groups, for example.

Age   10–16+ years.

Time

The preparation of the material might take about half an hour. The game itself should take a lesson.

N.B. It is advisable for the teacher to choose a poem with a distinctive metric pattern and rhyme scheme.

Recommended poems

'The Jumblies': Edward Lear
'The Listeners': Walter de la Mare   } younger pupils

'The Pied Piper': Robert Browning
'The Highwayman': Alfred Noyes   } 13–15 years

Sonnet 55: William Shakespeare
Verse 1 of 'Ode to Autumn': John Keats } 16+ years

3 IMAGINATIVE

Lucky dip

Aim

To encourage imaginative writing by offering a basic framework of objects and characters.

Requirements

Version One: Collections of pictures of faces, places and objects; 3 containers; paper and a pen for each pupil. Version Two: blackboard; paper and pens.

Method

VERSION ONE   The teacher should collect pictures of faces, places and objects in three different containers. The pupils could be asked to bring the pictures, but the teacher would be advised to have some in reserve.

Each pupil picks a face, a place and an object and writes a story round these three visual stimuli.

VERSION TWO   The teacher writes a list of incongruous objects on the blackboard, and asks the pupils to write a story which includes all these words. The pupils could make up the list before they have been told what the exercise is for,

e.g.: an elephant
a car
a bowl of custard
a toothbrush
a telegram

Age   9–13 years, especially slow learners.

Time   A lesson, possibly extended into homework.

Get out of this!

Aim

To provide the class with a stimulus for adventurous writing and to encourage their powers of quick, inventive thinking.

Requirements   Paper and a pen for each pupil.

Method

Arrange the class in pairs, then ask each pupil to describe a predicament at the top of their piece of paper,

e.g.: 'You are caught after dark by a policeman, riding a friend's bike with no lights and you discover you are travelling up a one-way street...' ending with the words 'Get out of this!'

  or 'You are stuck in a cave with your dog and your younger sister when you notice that the tide is coming in and it has cut off your route out... Get out of this!'

When each pupil has thought out and written down their predicament, the papers are exchanged within the pairs. The next pupil must then think of a way out of this predicament, and write it below. Then swap back the papers and read out the best examples.

Warning

Sometimes the pupils will think of situations that would be impossible even for Houdini. The exercise then becomes more imaginative and less realistic!

Age   9–12 years, especially slow learners.

Time   A lesson.

Plot and counterplot

Aim

To encourage pupils to co-operate in groups in making clear plans, and countering the plans of another group by thinking logically. This is a useful introduction to the concept of plot or storyline.

Requirements   Paper and a pen for each pupil.

Method

The class should be divided into small groups of about four or five.

STAGE ONE   Each group is detailed to make plans for committing a dastardly deed,

e.g.:   an art theft;
        an attempt to occupy an island or building;
        a bank robbery, etc.

The group should write out clear plans of their strategy, including maps, disguises, alibis, signals, etc.

STAGE TWO   Each group is then paired off with another group, and they exchange plans. All the groups then change their identity: They are no longer the criminals, but the detectors of crime. Each group must counter the plans in their hands by a written plan to foil the attempt.

STAGE THREE   When the counter-plans have been completed, the teacher should allow each group to discuss the plans and counter-plans with the paired group.

Age   9–12 years.

Time   Two lessons.

Sounds like...

Aim

To focus the pupils' attention on listening and identifying specific sounds; to increase their awareness that sound can add an important dimension to writing; and to stress that sound can be used as a stimulus for creative writing.

Requirements

All Variations: paper and a pen for each pupil. Variations One and Two: a tape of sound effects. Variations Three and Four: cassette tape recorders and tapes.

Method

VARIATION ONE   The pupils listen to a tape of sound effects. First, they attempt to identify the sounds. Then they try to recreate the sounds using letters, colours, shapes, etc., as well as words. Encourage them to use similes and metaphors to describe the sounds.

VARIATION TWO   The class listens to a tape of sound effects. They are asked to write a plausible story which incorporates the sound effects in the order in which they have been heard, with a rich description of each.

VARIATION THREE   Repeat Variation One but the pupils now prepare their own sound-effects tape in small groups.

VARIATION FOUR   Each of the pupils' tapes is given to another group who have to create a playscript which can use the sound effects tape as its sound tape in the order in which the sounds are given.

Each group of pupils can be encouraged to write their own radio play incorporating the dimension of sound.

Age   9–14 years.

Time

Variations One and Two: a lesson. Variations Three and Four: a more extended period of time.

Conversation

Aim

To build on dialogue-writing and develop narrative writing.

Requirements   Paper and a pen for each pupil.

Method

First, make sure that the class has learned how to set out dialogue correctly.

STAGE ONE   Ask the class to pick two incongruous characters, e.g. Mick Jagger and Queen Victoria, and write out an imaginary conversation between them.

STAGE TWO   For this extension of the game, each pupil should think of a specific place, e.g. Madame Tussaud's; the end of Brighton Pier, etc.

The more surreal the ideas, the more effective the writing, e.g. the dark side of the moon; at the pearly gates, etc.

Each pupil should then begin a longer piece of writing by describing the setting. The two characters must be introduced into that setting and they must engage in conversation.

The conversation can be lifted from the former game or an entirely new conversation can be constructed. Other characters can be introduced. The more bizarre the writing, the better it usually is.

Age   9–12 years.

Time   At least a lesson.

Dialogue

Aim

To base an imaginary conversation on real circumstances and emotions.

Requirements

Pupils should be asked to bring in magazines. Glue, scissors, paper and a pen for each pupil are also required.

Method

Ask the class to work in pairs. Each one of the pair cuts out a character or face which clearly expresses a particular emotion, and sticks the two together on to a piece of paper.

Each pair then makes up a plausible dialogue between the two characters and writes it out on a separate piece of paper.

The pictures and dialogues can be displayed around the classroom.

Variations

ORAL WORK   As above, but instead of the pair writing a dialogue between the characters they can improvise the imaginary situation.

This can be made more interesting if the teacher pins all the selected characters from magazines on to a wall of the classroom. Then, when the class watch each pair performing, they can attempt to guess which characters are being enacted.

Age   12–14 years.

Time   A lesson.

Points of view

Aim

To teach the difference between expressive and transactional writing.

Requirements   Paper and a pen for each pupil.

Method

The teacher should begin by talking about the difference between first person, expressive writing; and third person, transactional writing.

Then set up a situation, or series of situations, which could be described both ways. The pupils should write two accounts, using both techniques, making each as detailed and authentic as possible. One account should be a personalised interpretation and one should be an objective reportage.

SUGGESTED SCENARIOS   A fire in a department store: letter home/newspaper account. A car crash: letter to the offender/insurance report. A carnival: diary entry/police file.

Age   12–14 years.

Time   A lesson, with possible extension into homework.

Beginnings and endings

Aim

To help pupils think about the importance of the opening and the ending of a piece of writing.

Requirements

The teacher can contribute his or her own examples, or some of those from the list below.

Method

After talking about the importance of lively openings and memorable endings to pieces of written work, the teacher distributes small pieces of paper. Each pupil is then asked to write the opening sentence of an essay or story. These are then collected.

Then the teacher does the same with the final sentences, contributing their own or those below as well. Each pupil then picks an opening and an ending, and writes a story or essay using the opening and ending they have picked.

Age 13–16 years.

Time A lesson.

Beginnings

1 Algernon Forsyth was born with every material advantage in life, but with the serious disadvantage of being an odious and ill-tempered child.

2 As dawn broke the sky with flashes of orange, and a lone blackbird's song cut through the morning chill, George Loveday, shoes in hand, opened his own front door and tiptoed upstairs in his stockinged feet.

3 The end of the earth as we know it began on a beautiful, cloudless summer's day...

4 The telephone box must have been put up secretly in the middle of the night because as far as Mr Dawson knew, it wasn't in his garden the previous day.

Endings

1 But still the old swing creaked to and fro, to and fro, in the gusts of wind.

2 All that remained were the charred and smoking remains of the house.

3 As the spaceship cruised momentarily before increasing speed, David took a last glimpse of the familiar world he had grown up on.

4 Hillier realised that it was too late to tell people his story: no one would believe him anyway; he was alone on the African veldt apart from the circling shadows of the vultures above him.

Message in a bottle

Aim

To stimulate an organised response to a dilemma and to develop these ideas into an adventure story.

Requirements
Small pieces of paper and a pen for each pupil.

Method

Each pupil is asked to write a cryptic note to send off in a bottle asking for help. The pupil should decide where they are, in what sort of danger, and how much information to give on their note. The teacher then collects the messages and redistributes them.

Each pupil must then plan a campaign to rescue the person who sent the note. They should take notice of all the points of information that are given and create a plan around them.

This exercise can develop into an adventure story about the rescue attempt. The story could be further complicated by giving the pupils a list of hazards and pieces of good fortune. They could be asked to pick three or four of each and incorporate them into their extended story.

HAZARDS

1 The wind drops and you are becalmed.
2 You are doing the month's laundry and suddenly realise that you are in the middle of shark-infested waters.
3 Storm force 10 and increasing.
4 Compass error – you realise you are heading in the wrong direction.
5 You are sailing through unchartered waters with perilous reefs.
6 You encounter a ghost ship at dusk.
7 Sails are ripped in a storm and have to be repaired.
8 A bad case of sea-sickness!
9 Collision at night!
10 You run aground on a sandbank.

GOOD FORTUNE

1 Greeted by a school of friendly porpoises.
2 You put into harbour and are given a wonderful welcome by the islanders.

3 A fair wind and a course well set.

4 You rescue somebody from a sinking ship.

5 As relaxation you cast a line overboard and land a good catch.

6 Oysters for lunch reveal an interesting find.

7 Deck games fill in a lazy afternoon.

8 Diving competition from the decks of the ship.

9 Crossing the equator gives an opportunity for riotous games.

10 Scuba diving at an interesting coral reef.

Age 9–13 years.

Time This extended writing can take several lessons.

Dangerous journey

Aim

To stimulate exciting writing and exercise logical thinking in the planning of this writing.

Requirements   Paper and a pen for each pupil.

Method

Each pupil begins by taking one piece of paper and creating a character, and a quest or object for the character's journey, by answering the following questions, which can be put on the blackboard:

1 Name of a character
2 Brief physical description
3 Likes
4 Dislikes
5 Object of the quest
6 Area of the quest

The Character sheet might read like this:

1 Colonel Harry Blenkinsop
2 Monocle, wooden leg, red face, white hair
3 Likes: discipline, anecdotes, port, cigars, *The Times*
4 Dislikes: damp weather, soft drinks, punk rockers, television
5 He is seeking the place where he lost his leg.
6 On a mountain in the French Alps.

Taking a second sheet and now not thinking about the character of the quest, each pupil is asked to outline four possible disasters:

1 Technical failure: electric toothbrush goes wrong.
2 Natural disaster: earth tremor.
3 Man-made disaster: kidnapping.
4 Character failure: cowardice.

These Disaster sheets are collected in and each pupil is then asked to pick a sheet. Each pupil must plan a quest using his or her own character and quest, but incorporating the four disasters into the story in any order they wish to.

In order that the story is fully written, the teacher might wish to make a stipulation as to how much writing is required, e.g. one page of writing per disaster and one to introduce and one to conclude the story.

Age 9–12 years.

Time Two lessons.

Island in the sun

Aim

A game which encourages group work and decision-making in an imaginative context. It is also useful for reinforcing narrative and journalistic writing. It enables pupils to create and expand on the skeleton of a story.

Requirements

Paper and a pen for each pupil; felt-tip pens or coloured pencils, etc., for drawing.

Method

STAGE ONE (GROUP WORK)   The class is asked to form small groups. Each group is then asked to create an island of their own choice for them to live on. The group discusses, then writes briefly about their island, covering the following points:

1 The island's name
2 Its size
3 Its location
4 Description of inhabitants (if any)
5 Landscape
6 Climate
7 Vegetation
8 Animal life
9 Resources for survival

The group can also include an illustration of their island. Both the drawings and the written work are displayed for all the class to see.

STAGE TWO (INDIVIDUAL WORK)   Individually, each pupil writes a journal of the first week on the island, illustrating it if necessary.

Age   11–13 years.

Time   Several lessons.

Titanic

Aim

To encourage identification with a real historical character and situation, as an incentive to narrative writing.

Requirements

Paper and a pen for each pupil: character cards (see the list which follows).

Method

Give a brief outline of the *Titanic* disaster as follows:

The White Star Luxury Liner *Titanic* left Southampton on her maiden voyage to New York on 10 April 1912. Four days later on a calm, clear but cold Sunday night she struck a drifting iceberg.

This was a particularly tragic incident because the lifeboats were designed to carry 1178 passengers and on that fatal night there were 2207 passengers on board. Only 651 passengers survived.

Here follows a reconstructed log of the incident:

14 April

    11.40 p.m. Temperature at sea down to 31° Fahrenheit. *Titanic* collides with iceberg latitude 41 46′ N longitude 50 14′ W.

15 April

    12.05 a.m. Orders are given to uncover the boats, muster the crew and passengers.

    12.15 a.m. First wireless call for help.

    12.45 a.m. First distress rocket fired.

    12.45 a.m. First boat, No. 7, lowered.

    1.40 a.m. Last distress rocket fired.

    2.05 a.m. Last boat, collapsible D, lowered.

    2.10 a.m. Last wireless signals sent.

    2.18 a.m. Lights fail.

    2.20 a.m. Ship founders.

    3.30 a.m. *Carpathia*'s rockets sighted by boats.

4.10 a.m. First boat, No. 2, picked up by *Carpathia*.

8.30 a.m. Last boat, No. 12, picked up.

8.50 a.m. *Carpathia* heads for New York with 651 passengers.

Distribute character cards of the survivors at random to the class.

Each pupil should then tell their story of the disaster using the first person narrative voice, describing their survival from their character's point of view. The pupil should be encouraged to write in an idiom appropriate to their character.

Age 12–16 years.

Time A lesson.

Character Cards

Name	Age	Occupation	Cabin status
Roger Curtis	47	entertainments officer	Crew
Michael Stallard	50	laundry worker	Crew
Sir Edward Phelps	72	New York banker, retired	1st
Linda Wood	19	seamstress	3rd
Patricia Brown	40	nanny	2nd
Eric J. Wayman Jnr	39	property speculator	1st
Timothy 'Bimbo' Packer	34	professional golfer	1st
Lawrence Benbow	67	sea captain, retired	2nd
Catherine Poole	22	débutante	1st
Shelagh Douthwaite	20	millworker	3rd
Pamela Hawkins	42	guest house landlady	3rd
David Ridley	39	engineer	Crew
Martha Rodick	35	governess	3rd
Mary Shepherd	12	child	3rd
Antony Robinson	40	journalist	2nd
Michael Corr	17	waiter	Crew
Dame Anna Thomas	62	romantic novelist	1st
Margaret Haines	41	nurse	3rd
Ian Peveril	45	actor	1st

Ghislaine Forbes	36	tap dancer	3rd
Simon Forbes	42	wine taster	3rd
Maria Windo	43	opera singer	1st
David Hargrave	54	stoker	Crew
Heather Jenne	41	botanist	2nd
Michael Davies	47	boxing promoter	3rd
Andrew James	9	child	2nd
Jenny Smith	11	child	2nd
Katie Illingworth	10	child	2nd
Maximillian Noble	60	diamond merchant	1st
Jeremiah Popoff	20	Russian ballet dancer	1st
Gaie De Lapp	41	actress	1st

Paper darts

Aim

To help pupils to write instructions clearly and without ambiguity.

Requirements Paper and a pen for each pupil.

Method

Each pupil can make a paper dart, but how many could write clear instructions for making one?

Tell the class to imagine they are telling a visitor from Mars how to make the dart, with complete written instructions. Those who prefer to use diagrams may do so. Decide whether the pupils need to practise folding to remind themselves of the actions.

Then exchange instructions between pairs, to see if the instructions are accurate. Each pupil makes up a dart following their partner's instructions precisely. Only then can the darts be launched, to test the effectiveness of the instructions.

This game can be repeated with other forms of simple paper-folding, a paper boat or a paper hat, etc.

Age 9–11 years.

Time A lesson.

Subjective/objective

Aim

To understand the difference between these two methods of approach. This game is similar to 'Points of View' under Imaginative Writing, but is directed towards developing more functional skills.

Requirements   Paper and a pen for each pupil.

Method

1   THE SPOKEN METHOD   Arrange the class in pairs or ask them to arrange themselves.

Call one of each pair 'A' and the other 'B'. Choose a subject, e.g. a visit to the dentist; an accident, etc. Ask all 'A's to tell a story to the 'B's with as much personal observation as possible, i.e. a subjective account. Then ask the 'B's to retell the story to the 'A's giving the impersonal facts only, i.e. an objective account.

2   THE WRITTEN METHOD   Again organise the class into pairs.

Each pupil should begin by writing a report of a motor-cycle accident, for example, from the point of view of the rider, putting in as much subjective detail as possible. The pairs exchange stories and then become police officers who rewrite the story as a report in a clear, concise style.

The teacher can use this approach as a preliminary to newspaper study. The pupils can be directed to extract fact from opinion in articles or in advertisements.

Age   12–14 years.

Time   A lesson.

News-sheet

Aim

To practise writing to a given length, as a preparation for summary and editing work.

Requirements

Paper and a pen for each pupil; a list of possible topics as below.

Method

Give each pupil an aspect of school life (see list) to write about for a school information sheet. The article must not exceed 250 words.

The pupils then choose a partner and exchange articles. Both then assume the role of an editor who has to reduce the article to 100 words because of lack of space. Accuracy must also be checked by the editor.

Finished articles can be collected and made into a school news-sheet.

Age   13–15 years.

Time   A lesson.

Possible topics

assemblies	school meals
caretakers	school outings
drama productions	school rules
extra-curricular activities	school uniform
facilities	sport
going to camp	the curriculum
journey to and from school	the house system
library	the role of the school nurse
punishment systems	the school magazine
registration	the timetable
reports	

Headlines

Aim

To make pupils aware of the distinctive requirements of journalistic writing, and editing skills.

Requirements

A collection of newspaper headlines, assembled by the class or the teacher.

Method

STAGE ONE   The teacher can collect together sensational headlines or the pupils can be asked to make this collection themselves before the lesson. The headlines are put in a box or hat and each pupil picks one out.

The class are then asked to write an article in journalistic style to go with their headlines. The length should be specified: say 150 words. The articles can be edited by the teacher or other pupils and collected into newspaper form.

STAGE TWO   The pupils are asked to take a partner and exchange articles. Each pupil then becomes the sub-editor who has to cut the article back to no more than 100 words.

STAGE THREE   The sub-editors could then think of a headline and see how this differs from the original headline.

Finally, ask the sub-editors to write one short paragraph for the front page of the newspaper, paraphrasing the entire story the readers will find inside.

Age   14–16 years.

Time   A lesson or several lessons.

Accident claim

Aim

To practise the language of form-filling, by answering briefly and succinctly.

Requirements
Two pieces of paper and a pen for each pupil.

Method

Each pupil is asked to describe a car accident for the purposes of an insurance claim, in a fixed number of words.

The 'forms' are then collected in and redistributed. The new recipient now assumes the identity of the insurance officer, and writes out a recommendation to their superior for further investigations, immediate payment, etc. according to its convincing detail.

Age
16–18 years.

Time
At least a full lesson.

Travel brochure

Aim

To try writing in the concise but alluring style of a travel brochure.

Requirements

Old travel brochures (available from most travel firms); paper, pens and pencils for each pupil.

Method

The class should begin by studying the brochures for style.

The pupils then divide into pairs and, using the brochure as a model, invent their own to advertise a tour, including a detailed itinerary for seven days and nights. The brochure should include information about costs, transport, places to be visited, likely climate, etc.

Age 13–15 years.

Time A lesson.

READING

This chapter is divided into two parts; the first part offers games which aim to develop the different skills which make up reading ability; the second part is based on a broader understanding of literature.

So many assumptions are made about reading that, once a child has been declared 'able to read', often little is done by the teacher to refine that skill. Yet different kinds of reading ability are needed to cope with different types of activity. These games might help to distinguish and develop these requirements.

Once a pupil is able to read, English teachers will encourage a wide exploration of literature. They will also expect some kind of response to that literature. The games included in the second section could be used to add variety to the quality of that response.

Say it aloud

Aim

To practise reading aloud to an audience, and to test listening comprehension.

Requirements

In advance of the lesson, the teacher asks each pupil to find a short passage of particular interest to them from a magazine or newspaper, etc.,

e.g.: a short passage on fishing; a review of a pop concert or record, etc.

The pupils prepare their passages for reading aloud, and also think of six questions on the content.

Method

The teacher should advertise well in advance when the pupils will be expected to bring their prepared passages

In small groups, each pupil in turn is called upon to read their passage while the others in the group listen attentively. The reader will then ask the prepared questions to the group to test their listening ability.

The procedure is repeated until everyone in the group has had a turn at reading.

Age   9–13 years.

Time   A lesson.

Use your library

Aim

To make pupils familiar with the organisation of the library, and increase their knowledge of bibliography.

Requirements

The lesson should be spent in the library. Copies of activity lists are needed (see below).

Method

The teacher should prepare in advance a number of question sheets on different sections of the library. Since libraries obviously differ in their contents, we include just two sample sets of questions below.

Hand out the sheets to pairs of pupils, and make sure that everyone starts at a different point to avoid bunching over one shelf.

Age   9–12 years.

Time   A lesson.

Where do I find...?

Find the Dewey classification numbers from the book spines of non-fiction books on the following subjects:

1 VOLCANOES... (551.2)

2 NEW HORIZONS IN ASTRONOMY... (520)

3 ROMAN ART... (704)

4 EVERYDAY LIFE IN THE NEW TESTAMENT... (220.95)

5 THE POLICE... (363)

6 BUDDHA... (294)

7 COSTUME FOR THE STAGE... (391)

8 MUSIC... (780)

9 CLOWNS... (791)

Fiction

1 What novels did Nina Bawden write?

2 Who published the novels of Bernard Ashley?

3 How many different 'Lawrences' are there with novels on the shelves of your library?

4 In what year was *Heidi* first published? What is the name of the translator?

5 List the authors in the fiction section whose surnames begin with Z.

6 In which order on the shelves should you find the following novelists: John Wyndham; Evelyn Waugh; Barbara Willard; Robert Westall; H. G. Wells?

7 Who wrote *I am the Cheese*, and what other novels did he write?

8 How many books by John Christopher are there on the shelves at the moment? List the titles in the order in which they were published.

9 What books by Roald Dahl are being read by pupils in your school at the moment?

10 How many times has *The Owl Service* by Alan Garner been reprinted? How many times has *Black Jack* by Leon Garfield been reprinted?

Readability

Aim

To make pupils aware of the effect of type-size, spacing, etc. on their ability to read and comprehend.

Requirements

Examples of good and bad typography brought in by the teacher.

Method

Start with the two examples below. Which advertisement do the pupils find easier to understand, and why? Can they isolate the different features of the display?

Ask the pupils to bring in their own examples of readable and unreadable type. Then ask them to design their own advertisement or poster for an event, featuring in a clear relationship: the subject; the date; the time; the venue; the price of tickets, etc.

Age   9–12 years or less able pupils.

Time   A lesson.

For comparison

1 Which catches your attention best?

2 Which gives you more information?

3 Which one makes you want to follow it up?

Patterns of print

Aim

To encourage pupils to focus on the visual dimension of print as well as the interest of words and phrases juxtaposed. The game may begin in a random way but ends with the pupils engaged in selecting and organising material.

Requirements

The teacher and the class should all collect different kinds of printed material. The material should be cut into words or phrases and kept in a large box; card; glue; scissors.

Method

Pupils can work in pairs or individually. Each pair or pupil selects ten pieces of print of different visual types. They then organise and arrange the phrases or words to create visual patterns and juxtapositions, as well as patterns and contrasts of meaning.

The phrases and words can then be arranged and stuck to pieces of card; words can be added to link up pieces of print if necessary. Each piece can be given a title, and illustrations of a printed or original nature can be added. The results can be displayed.

Age   9–13 years.

Time

It will take time to collect the material together, but the game itself will only take a lesson.

In the news

Aim

To develop speedy reading for information purposes; to be aware of the arrangement and bias of a newspaper.

Requirements

Two copies each of several newspapers, national or local.

Method

The class is divided into pairs, each with identical newspapers. Each pupil takes it in turns to ask the other questions about different pages in their paper,

e.g.: 1 Who was 'smiling through the rain'? (The Queen)

2 Who won the 3.30 at Doncaster?

3 What's on Channel 4 at 9.30 tonight?

4 What does the editor think about the threatened miners' strike?

The teacher should aim to encourage the pupils to progress from straight location and comprehension questions to questions of bias and emphasis.

Age 13–14 years.

Time A lesson.

Flotsam and jetsam

Aim

To teach pupils to vary their speeds of reading, from quick skimming to considered reflection.

Requirements

Copies of an informative passage of writing, to which every pupil has access; paper and pens for each pupil.

Method

STAGE ONE   Explain to the class that they are going to skim-read the passage for one minute. Obviously they will not read every word in it, but the should attempt to skim over the whole to grasp the general sense of it.

The class does this, and when the minute is up, the passages are turned over while the teacher asks general questions about the passage. The teacher can thus find out what impression the class has gleaned about subject matter, point of view, etc.

STAGE TWO   The class is divided into small groups and re-reads the passage more carefully. They then discuss and attempt to resolve between them the point of the passage, its scope and approach.

STAGE THREE   Finally, in pairs, the pupils should write a summary of the main points of the passage.

Age   13–16 years.

Time   A lesson.

Let your fingers do the walking

Aim

To develop reference skills, in preparation for 'life skills'.

Requirements

As many copies of the Yellow Pages as possible. Paper and pens for the class; copies of the list below.

Method

Ask the class to bring in copies of the Yellow Pages. and share them round.

The game can be played in two different ways:

1 The teacher reads out the problems one at a time, and the class race each other to find the solution to each one before the next problem is given.

2 The teacher gives the pupils the full sheet and they are asked to write in the answers on the sheet. The first one finished and checked as correct is the winner.

Age

This game can be used either to practise quick reading and reference skills from 11 upwards, or for real practice in life skills for 15–16 year olds.

Time   A lesson.

Sample questions

Pupils are asked to give a name and telephone number in answer to the following problems:

1 Who would you phone if you had rats in your house?

2 Who would you phone if you had a broken bedstead which needed disposal?

3 Who would you phone if you had a lot of old wine bottles to dispose of?

4 ...you want to give blood?

5 ...you had a dead cow in the garden?

6 ...you want someone to print invitations?

7 ...you want to find out about adult evening classes?

8 ...you want to buy a tractor?

9 ...you want to charter a plane?

10 ...you want to rent a space invaders machine?

11 ...you want your driveway resurfaced?

12 ...you want to hire a video?

13 ...you want to repair your 'Black & Decker'?

14 ...your foundations are cracking?

15 ...you have blocked drains?

16 ...you want to rent a car?

This list can be added to.

Spotlight

Aim

To provide an imaginative way of personifying the characters in a novel.

Requirements   That the class will have read a novel together.

Method

Ask for volunteers who would be prepared to represent characters from the book at a special press conference.

The rest of the class who do not volunteer for particular roles are journalists and must prepare to ask questions. They must also take notes during the conference. Finally they must write either a feature or an account of the interview for their paper.

The characters should sit at the front of the class and announce their identity, then the rest of the class take it in turns to question a chosen character not on what happened to them in the book but questions which demand a more imaginative response,

e.g.: 'What did you feel when you thought you'd been deserted by the rats in the kitchen, Mrs Frisby?'

While the journalists are writing up their accounts for the papers, the characters can write their own 'inside' stories.

All the articles can be collected and displayed.

Age   11–15 years.

Time   At least one lesson: it could develop.

Face to face

Aim

To stimulate a creative response to literature which encourages an understanding of the characters and the author's intentions.

Requirements

That each pupil selects a novel they have read; paper and a pen for each pupil.

Method

The class has to imagine that they are chosen characters in their books. The pupils must write as that character about their role within the book. This could include perceptions of themselves and their personality, as felt by the character; what the character thinks should hold the reader's attention; what the character thinks are the important ideas discussed in the novel, and so on.

For example, one pupil has read Hardy's *Far from the Madding Crowd* and chooses the character of Gabriel Oak. The pupil writes in an appropriately simple style. Perhaps Gabriel could cite the parts of the story where he thought the reader was moved; when he lost his sheep; when Bathsheba dismissed him; but also he might suggest that he felt the reader lost sympathy for him when he displayed excessive loyalty and dependability, etc.

Age

This can be a very sophisticated game, suitable for the most able pupils. At its own level, it is successful for candidates at any stage from CSE to 'O' or 'A' Level standard. 14–16 years.

Time   Several lessons.

Meet my maker

Aim

To think about books as artifices and to understand the author's intentions and plan.

Requirements

The class must all have read and studied the same novel.

Method

VARIATION ONE: WRITTEN FORM   Each pupil is asked to take one of the characters from the book and prepare a list of questions that that character might like to ask the author, the creator. These should be questions about why certain things happened in the book and not questions outside the scope of the book,

e.g.: The class might have read *Kes* by Barry Hines. One pupil might pick out the character of Billy Casper. Billy might like to know:

1 Why did Jud kill the hawk?

2 Why did my dad leave home?

3 Why is Jud always bullying me?

The next stage is for the pupil to adopt the voice and character of the author. They must try to thing about the author's intentions and provide and answer their own questions,

e.g.: *Billy:* Why did Jud kill the hawk?
Barry Hines: Jud was furious about the bet, resentful of Billy having something to love. Also I wanted a dramatic and tragic climax to my book.

VARIATION TWO: ORAL FORM   The game can be played in oral form where one pupil might volunteer to be Billy Casper and another to be Barry Hines. They could either have an improvised conversation in front of the class or the questions and answers could be talked about beforehand.

Age

A more difficult game suitable for older pupils, 14 upwards. It could be useful for those studying literature for examination purposes, for CSE, 'O' Level or even 'A' Level.

Time   Two lessons.

This is your life

Aim To revitalise a familiar play or novel.

Requirements

That the class should have read a play or novel together.

Method

If the class is large, split it into two groups. Each group can then operate in the same way. The groups are told that they are going to prepare a *This Is Your Life* programme on the central character in a play or novel, e.g. Billy from *Billy Liar*.

One person should volunteer to be Billy Liar, and one pupil should be the compère. Each other member of the group must pick either a character from the play, such as Rita, Barbara, Arthur, Grandma, Mr Shadrack, etc.; or an imaginary character such as Billy's primary school teacher, Barbara's mum, etc.

Each character should prepare a short anecdote about Billy, in the appropriate language and style for that character. Meanwhile, Billy and the compère prepare and write the format, leaving spaces for each character.

When the scenario is ready the performance should be practised before each group performs their piece in front of the other group.

Age 14–15 years.

Time At least two lessons.